"Funny. Healing. Thoroughly attention-grabbing. Peek into Rick Hamlin's transparent prayer life and the prayers of many others such as Corrie Ten Boom, Catherine Marshall, and Mother Teresa."

—MARION BOND WEST, author of *Praying for My Life*

"If you find yourself struggling with prayer, as many people do, Rick Hamlin's *10 Prayers You Can't Live Without* is here to liberate you. Through anecdotes from *Guideposts* readers and the wisdom he has acquired from a lifetime of praying, Hamlin shows how prayer can become an effortless conversation with God. And he does so in a humorous, inspiring, and poignant way. Highly recommended!"

—MARCIA FORD, author of *The Indispensable Guide to Practically Everything: Prayer*

"I love this book! I pray that you will read it and experience the power of prayer in your life."

—JON GORDON, author of *The Energy Bus* and *The Seed*

"Rick Hamlin is a praying man for whom praying is as natural as breathing. In the years I've known him, I've often asked myself how he does it. Now I've got an answer. Rick's amazing book *10 Prayers You Can't Live Without* is full of bold insight and practical wisdom about the practice that is the very breath of our spiritual lives. The fact is the more I learn about Rick, the more I learn about prayer."

—EDWARD GRINNAN, editor-in-chief of *Guideposts* and author of *The Promise of Hope*

"Here are ten words to describe *10 Prayers You Can't Live Without*: charming, inspiring, liberating, delightful, engrossing, moving, wise, healing, thoughtful, beautiful."

—BOB HOSTETLER, author of *How to Survive the End of the World*

"Prayer has long been, for me, more a source of worry than of comfort or strength. I don't pray as often as I'd like or as meaningfully. With insights and instruction woven almost invisibly through his little compendium of prayer stories, Rick Hamlin not only transformed my prayer habits but banished my insecurities about prayer. 'To try to pray is to pray,' he reassures in the very first sentence. By the end of his book, under his gentle tutelage, I was trying all the time."

—PATTY KIRK, author of *The Gospel of Christmas* and *A Field Guide to God*

"Whether you're a newcomer to prayer or a lifelong prayer warrior encountering an occasional dry spell, *10 Prayers You Can't Live Without* is a book you can't live without. From his own daily appointment with God on the subway to the experiences of people he knows— both famous and unknown—Rick Hamlin has distilled guidelines to make every prayer a true 'conversation with God.'"

—ELIZABETH SHERRILL, author of *All the Way to Heaven*

# 10

# Prayers
# You Can't
# Live Without

# 10 Prayers You Can't Live Without

## How to Talk to God About Everything

### RICK HAMLIN

HAMPTON ROADS

Cover design by Jim Warner

Hampton Roads Publishing Company, Inc.
Charlottesville, VA 22906
Distributed by Red Wheel/Weiser, LLC
*www.redwheelweiser.com*

Sign up for our newsletter and special offers by going to *www.redwheelweiser.com/newsletter/.*

ISBN: 978-1-57174-741-9

Library of Congress Control Number: 2016930212

Printed in the United States of America

M&G

10 9 8 7 6 5 4 3 2 1

For Sweetie

Ques. pg. 242

# CONTENTS

Contents

# INTRODUCTION

To try to pray is to pray.

You can't fail at it. Nobody can. Open your heart, open your mouth, say something, say nothing. Shout if you must. Raise your hands, clasp them in your lap. Sing if you please. You can start with a "Dear Lord" and end with an "Amen," or you can dive right in. You can close your eyes, get on your knees, use whatever language you like or no language at all. You can pray when you're walking, running, driving to work, setting the table for dinner, lying in bed before you turn the light out.

To try it is to do it. It's the only human endeavor I can think of where trying is doing. Reaching out is holding on. Joining in is letting go. Prayer is as natural as breathing. It's fun. It's a relief. It's comforting. It's a solace. You can tell yourself it's an obligation or that it's a terrific waste of time, but how often do you get to waste time with a purpose? If you're like me and think every minute of your day has to be accounted for, you really do need prayer. You'll run out of steam without it.

You can do it in private. You can do it with a friend at your kitchen table or in a church pew or with your family at dinner. You can do it in a windowless basement with a twelve-step group or out under the stars on a summer night. You can practice it all you like, but the practice itself is perfect. No need for a dress rehearsal. All your false attempts, your back-up-and-try-again efforts—they're it.

You will wonder if you're doing it right. You will want a little more guidance. You'll want to hear from others who take it seriously and learn from their example. Even the finest cooks look for inspiration in a new cookbook. But the masters will affirm that prayer is a school for amateurs because doing it from the heart is all that matters. That's the only expertise you need.

For thirty years I've made a conscious effort to work on my prayer life. I do it religiously, faithfully, absentmindedly. I often forget to pray, but I don't forget how. I don't think you really can. A need, a friend, a worry, a piece of bad news or a cause for celebration pulls me back. Returning is part of the process. So is waiting. Besides, being critical of your prayers defeats the whole purpose.

What has helped me? The Bible, especially the Psalms. A faith community that challenges me and keeps me on my toes—Sundays at church, I get recharged. Writers who know more than I do. Friends who give me working models of passionate faith. A family that prayed together and still does at every dinner. And for almost all those thirty years I've worked for a magazine where I've been expected to ask boldly, sometimes brazenly, about other people's prayer lives.

"Do you ever pray?" I ask, or "When did you pray?" or "Did you pray about that?" You'd be surprised by the answers and how committed people are to prayer. I remember the actress whom I had written off as a spiritual lightweight because she showed up in glossy fashion magazines. "I pray all the time," she said without a pause. Or there was the newscaster who spoke profoundly and humbly of the people in disasters she prayed for, disasters she had to report on. "Easy enough for you to say," I thought, until I discovered quite by accident how she followed up those prayers with substantial financial help. (No, I can't say who she was. Giving anonymously was a crucial part of her faith.) And there have been the countless subjects who have promised to put me in their prayers. One recently e-mailed me because she had a sense that I needed urgent prayer. (She was right.)

To tune into people's prayers is to look into their souls. It's to learn how to love them and stretch my own soul. Through my job I've heard the prayers of farmers battling drought, athletes pushed to their physical limits, people dealing with disease and financial turmoil and incalculable loss. I can't begin to say what an effect all these stories have had on me except to give you a glimpse of the ones that I still retell myself.

I've called this book *Ten Prayers You Can't Live Without* because it's an attempt to break down and categorize the prayers I find the most helpful. Do I expect you to pray exactly the prayers that I have in the same way? Goodness no. Prayer is personal. Find the way that works best for you. Even the Lord's Prayer can be said in different ways. I hope I can expand your thinking about it and help you find other prayers to use. There's "Nooooooooo!" and "Thanks" and "Forgive me, I blew it" and "Hi, God!" At other times I turn to more formal prayers like the one a mentor taught me: "Jesus Christ, have mercy upon me. Make haste to help me. Rescue me and save me. Let thy will be done in my life."

As I said, we're all amateurs at prayer. You can practice a prayer in your head, like a conversation you expect to have with your boss. You want to get the words right. You want to make sure you're understood. But don't forget that every thought you've phrased and rephrased in your mind has been heard and understood better than you could have expressed it.

"Search me, O God, and know my heart," the psalmist says. "Try me and know my thoughts."

Every writer hopes to be read, but I would be just as happy if you stopped reading me, dog-eared a page or marked a spot in your e-reader and prayed instead. A doctor I interviewed once told me that for him, reading was a form of prayer. I believe that. Would that reading this book feels like prayer to you (writing it certainly has been for me). A good read makes me want to talk to the author. But in this case if you talked to our Maker, I would feel like I really accomplished something.

# CHAPTER ONE

# Pray at Mealtime

---◆◇◆---

*"Bless this food to our use, us to your service,
and bless the hands that prepared it."*

It all started with a nightly blessing.

My father's rambling graces were famous in the neighborhood. Whenever one of us invited a friend over for dinner we usually warned, "Dad always starts dinner with a prayer. Just bow your head. Don't eat anything until Dad says amen.

"And it might take him a while to get there."

I was one of four kids, each of us two years apart. We lived in an LA suburb that looked like any suburb we saw on TV. Our street was lined with palm trees that wrapped themselves around my kites. We had rosebushes in front, an orange tree and a flowering pear that dropped white petals in January like snow. The flagstone walk was lined with yellow pansies leading to a red front door.

We ate dinner in a room Mom insisted on calling the lanai. It had once been a back porch and had been converted with the help of plate glass, sliding glass doors, screens and a corrugated fiberglass roof that made a tremendous racket when the rain hit it. But this was Southern California so it wasn't often.

Dad came in from his commute on the freeway, kissed Mom, hung up his jacket, poured himself a drink, checked out the news on TV. One of us kids set the table. Mom took the casserole out of the oven with big orange pot holders and set it on the counter. "Ta-da!" she exclaimed. She tossed the salad in a monkey pod bowl they had picked up on a trip to Hawaii. "Dinner!" she called in her high-pitched, musical voice. "Dinner's ready."

We converged on the lanai from different parts of the house, my sisters from their rooms upstairs or the sewing room where my older sister, Gioia, was always re-hemming a skirt in the constant battle of fashion vs. school rules. I seem to remember a three-by-five card being slid between the floor and the bottom of her skirts when she was kneeling. The hem had to touch the card or the girls' vice principal would send her home. My older brother and I slept in a converted garage, which was convenient for whatever motor vehicle he was working on. Howard could roll the minibike or go-cart right into the room from the driveway. No steps to climb. I slept with the familiar smell of gasoline, and my brother had to put up with the old upright piano next to my bed.

We were as different as two boys could be. He never held a tool he didn't know how to use. I never heard a Broadway show that I didn't want to learn the lyrics to. He was physical, mechanical. He could fix anything. He was outdoors racing the minibike up and down the driveway with his neighborhood fan base cheering him on. I was inside, listening to a new LP, learning a song inside my head. I was overly sensitive. He pretended to be thick-skinned.

It's a wonder we didn't pummel each other, although as the older brother by twenty-two months, he pummeled me enough. I didn't circulate in his orbit. Not even close. Howard would wake me up early in the morning to go work on one of his forts and I would find an excuse to return to the house to work on a watercolor. Sometimes we had great talks as we were falling asleep. Most of the time, though, we did our own thing, Howard soaking an engine part in a Folgers coffee can of motor oil, me studying the liner notes for a record album.

Then came the blessing.

Dad's graces were a call to worship, an effort to pull these disparate family members together, to get us all on the same page. We gathered at the big teak table and the dog was sent outside to bark. We squirmed, we giggled, we kicked each other under the table, we rolled our eyes, but we were forced to see that we were all one and we had to be silent for a minute or two. We scraped our chairs against the linoleum floor (eventually it was covered with a lime-green indoor-outdoor carpet). We left homework, the kite caught in the tree, the news on TV, the seat for the minibike, the Simplicity pattern laid out on the floor, the rolls in the oven. We rushed in from school meetings and play practice and afterschool jobs. My younger sister, Diane, put her hamster Hamdie back in his cage and we could hear the squeak of the animal running to nowhere on his wheel.

"Let us reflect on the day," Dad began. We closed our eyes.

Then he paused.

There was a whole world in that pause. Silence. Nothing to do but think. I have been in Quaker meetings where we sat in silence waiting for the Spirit to move and it was just like that pause. I have worshipped in churches where the minister was wise enough to be quiet for a moment as soon as we bowed our heads. Every Monday in our office we gather in a conference room at 9:45 and read prayer requests that have come in to us over the past week; then we close our eyes, pausing in silence before we remember those requests.

At first all you hear is ambient noise. The drone of an air conditioner, the hum of a computer, a car passing by, my sister's hamster squeaking in his cage, your stomach rumbling. You think, "That hamster wheel needs some WD-40....That car needs a new muffler....Boy, I'm hungry." Then you listen to what's going on in your head.

Back then my head was spinning with a million thoughts. I was replaying what my best friend and I had talked about under the walnut tree at school or what Miss McGrath had said about my paper in class or what I wished I could say to the cute girl who sat behind me. What I wished she thought about me. Reflect on the day? There was too much noise going on inside. What did that have to do with prayer?

All we had to do was listen to Dad. Like a great preacher warming up, he cleared his throat and began, usually with something he heard on the radio or saw on TV.

"God, I ask you to be with us in the coming election," he prayed. "May the voters make the right choices in the primary."

"Remember our president as he makes his State of the Union address.

"Be with our astronauts in tomorrow's flight.

"Remember the Dodgers in tonight's playoffs.

"We are sorry about those who suffered from the recent tornadoes.

"We mourn the death of your servant Dr. Martin Luther King."

"It's like the six o'clock news," one of my brother's friends said. "You don't need the radio or the TV. You can get all the headlines from your dad's grace at dinnertime." Prayer can be a way of conveying information. It can be the means of processing history, even recent history. Think of all those passages in the Psalms that rehash the Israelites wandering in the desert: "Forty years long was I grieved with this generation, and said, It is a people that do err in their heart, and they have not known my ways: Unto whom I sware in my wrath that they should not enter into my rest" (Psalm 95:10, KJV).

A modern-day psalmist in a button-down shirt and a bowtie, Dad prayed us through the 1960s and 1970s, the Watts riots, the flower power of Haight-Ashbury, the turmoil of the Vietnam War, the stock market's rise and fall, inflation, Kent State, Cambodia, Watergate, Nixon, Agnew, Ford, Carter. Dad dumped everything in his prayers, all the noise in his head, all the stuff he worried about. They were throw-everything-in-but-the-kitchen-sink prayers.

Let me extol the benefit of such prayers. First of all, this is a *great* way of dealing with the news.

I have friends who get so riled up about what they've seen on TV or read on the Internet or in the paper that they can't sleep at night.

The first moment you see them you have to let them unload, let them chill. "I can't believe what a terrible trap our president has got us into," they'll exclaim, or "Congress is ruining our nation" or "I just read a terrible story about corruption in government." They're so anxious that you can't have a normal conversation until they've let go of their worries.

Of course, the news can be devastating. The headline splashed across the front of a newspaper in bold type sends a chill through me. The nightmarish scenario on the TV news has me double-locking the doors and tossing and turning at night. But most of those news stories were crafted to make us scared. Fear sells newspapers and magazines. The cover line about the ten most dangerous toys that can hurt your children makes you want to pick up that parenting magazine at the supermarket checkout. Fear about how your house might have a poisonous noxious gas seeping into it keeps you glued to the TV. Scary Internet headlines are designed to make you click through. You're supposed to get upset.

I do. All the time. If I read too much bad news it puts me in a foul mood. Talk about controlling my thoughts. I once stared at a provocative headline in a tabloid at a newsstand and screamed right back at it. My nerves were jangled. Something about the wording set me off there at Madison and 34th Street, right around the corner from the office. I was so shocked I slunk away hoping no one had heard me. Who was that jerk making all that noise? What got into me? The tabloid could have winked and smiled back at me: *Gotcha!*

Bad news can become a dangerous loop in my head. It's usually about stuff I have no control over: the national debt, the unemployment rate, the decline of the dollar, war, the weather, the poverty level, the stock market, the trade imbalance, the decline of the West, the decline of civility, growing pollution, the polar ice cap melting. It's essential to be well informed. I'm a junkie for all kinds of news. Good thing all those reporters and columnists keep me up-to-date. But there's no reason for the bad news to consume me.

If the news pulls you down it can rob you of the creativity you need to get your best work done. A study has shown that getting your blood pressure up by reading a depressing story in the newspaper or watching a disturbing report on television prevents your mind from doing the intuitive wandering it needs to make creative connections. That sounds like the work of prayer to me (and no, the article didn't put it that way). Save the news for times when your mind doesn't have to be at its best. Or take it in early and then toss it away.

Dad put the news back into God's hands. He asked God to intervene in places God was not necessarily considered. What did God know about the Dow and runaway inflation? What would God think about Nixon and Watergate? The point was, if we were thinking about it, the good Lord deserved to hear it. The good Lord would care.

As Dad's graces continued, he moved on to matters closer to home.

"We look forward to seeing our daughter Gioia march in the drill team at the football game tonight, bless her," he prayed.

"Bless Rick at the piano recital on Sunday."

"We're grateful for the new minibike Howard bought. We pray that he uses it safely and ask him to receive your blessing."

"We're thankful for Diane's good tennis match today."

"We look forward to Back to School Night and meeting our children's teachers. We know you know what good work they do. Bless them."

What a valuable lesson in prayer and parenting. Dad prayed for us. He noticed what was going on in our lives. Not the secrets that lurked inside, like my crush on the girl who sat behind me in fifth grade, but the events that were on his radar. The football game, the homecoming parade, the senior class musical, a tennis tournament, finals, dance class, the prom. He paid attention. At Back to School Night he graded our teachers and came back home to tell us how they measured up, which was to say how we measured up. He wrote it all down on a piece of paper with letter grades. When he gave my fourth-grade teacher, Miss McCallum, an A, I felt like the luckiest kid on earth. You can never underestimate a child's need for love and attention from his parents.

Francis McNutt, the great advocate for healing prayer, would often ask when he spoke to groups how many people remembered their parents praying for them. How many had heard their mother or father pray for them when they were sick, for instance? How many remembered a time when a parent had prayed out loud for them? Maybe twenty percent could recall a moment when their moms had prayed for them, but their dads? Only three percent of them.

I read that figure in astonishment, wondering how my father managed it, especially for a man of his generation, a buttoned-up World War II submarine veteran, the suffer-in-silence type. How did he ever learn to open up like this to us? How did he get over the natural embarrassment that comes from praying out loud in front of your loved ones? I'm far more the wear-it-on-my-sleeve sort, and even I fumble when I have to pray extemporaneously with my family. For Dad it came as naturally as breathing. There must have been something healing in it for him, blessing us and dinner every night.

I thought of Dad's graces recently when we ran a story about a dad, Kevin Williamson, who, with his two teenagers, was celebrating his first Thanksgiving after his wife, Bev, had died of cancer.

Kevin didn't want to get out of bed that morning, let alone celebrate. Long before his children were up, he trudged into the kitchen and got a cup of tea. The only sound was the rumble of the refrigerator. The quiet time reminded him of Bev and the mornings they had spent planning their days and their future, a future that had turned out different from what he'd ever imagined. The phone rang. It was their neighbor who was having them over to dinner. "Can I bring anything?" he asked.

"Just yourselves," she said. "And bread...we could use some bread."

"Sure." He figured he'd go out and buy some at whatever supermarket was open. Then his eye landed on his wife's recipe box still sitting on the counter. He thought of Bev's yeast rolls, the same recipe that had been handed down in his own family for generations. His mother had taught Bev to make them. He could remember the scent of them wafting from the wood-burning stove at his great-grandmother's home.

Kevin found the recipe card, written in his own mother's handwriting. He put on an apron, got out a mixing bowl and lined up the ingredients on the counter.

"What are you making?" his daughter asked, wandering into the kitchen sleepy-eyed.

"Mom's yeast rolls." He stirred the yeast into warm water, beat an egg, added the flour, kneaded the dough and let it rise. He separated the dough in balls and put them on a baking sheet. Perfect for dinner. But there was still some left over.

Bev had always made an early batch just for the family. Maybe he could do the same. With the leftover dough he made a few more rolls and put them in the oven. Soon the kitchen smelled like all those Thanksgivings of the past. He thought of Bev, how she made her family laugh, how she taught them to love and to live. The timer buzzed. He took the pan out of the oven, then called his kids into the kitchen.

"Let's all have one," he said, putting the rolls on a plate.

They sat at the kitchen table and joined hands, and he bowed his head to say grace. "God, it's been a tough year for us. We miss Bev so much. We thank you for the time we had with her. We're grateful for the little reminders, each day, of her presence in our lives still. And we're blessed that we have one another."

The story was from Kevin's point of view, not the kids', but I don't doubt they were suffering the loss of their mom just as acutely and were comforted by their dad's grace. They knew they had been loved and still were.

My dad's prayers were filled with his love for us and for Mom. He prayed for President Nixon, the astronauts, Sandy Koufax and *us*. We were on equal footing with the famous people who dominated the news. We were stars. What he couldn't always articulate in a conversation he could say in a prayer. He bowed his head and his heart opened up. He told us the good things he thought of us.

Dad was a far more complicated person than my straightforward, sunny-tempered mother. He worried more, hurt more, suffered more and internalized most of it. He smoked, he drank—the clink of ice cubes in a glass was an enduring part of the soundtrack of my childhood. He could be self-involved. He got angry and didn't know how to express the anger. He could burst out in a frightening tirade, most often directed against himself. The sound of Dad throwing his tennis racket against the fence and chastising himself—"Thornt!!"—was a familiar feature of Sunday's mixed doubles with Mom. You could tell which rackets were his in the hall closet because they were usually bent or patched up with tape. But in his prayers he loved and was lovable.

From Dad's graces I picked up a tool I use almost every day when I pray. It's one of the most valuable things I know and it was a long time before I recognized how helpful it was.

When you close your eyes to pray and start listening to your heart, you're going to face a slew of distractions. You'll hear a kid bouncing a basketball down the sidewalk, a radiator will rattle, a bus's brakes will squeak. You'll start thinking of all the stuff you need to get accomplished that day, and soon you'll exclaim, "Geez, what am I doing? I haven't prayed at all."

Dad's graces were frequently interrupted. Our dog Andy barked. The next-door neighbor's dog barked. The phone rang. A passing car honked. Mom's kitchen timer went off. We started to giggle.

Dad put the interruptions right into the prayer:

"God, be with our dog Andy. Help him protect us."

"Thank you for our daughter's popularity. We know that whoever is calling for her will call back." In case Gioia hadn't dashed to the phone already.

"Bless Mom's rolls in the oven. We look forward to eating them." In case Mom hadn't gone to get them.

"Bless our children's high spirits. You know their energy is a good thing."

If you fight an interruption in a prayer, it becomes much bigger. If you fold it into the prayer loop, it becomes part of the weave of your thoughts, the cord that becomes your lifeline. Even monks who devoted hours to meditation, star athletes in the spiritual life, get distracted in prayer.

Thomas Merton, the brilliant writer and Trappist monk at the Abbey of Gethsemani in Kentucky, wrote one of the greatest modern prayers of spiritual yearning: "My Lord God, I have no idea where I am going. I do not see the road ahead of me. I cannot know for certain where it will end. Nor do I really know myself, and the fact that I think I am following your will does not mean that I am actually doing so. But I believe that the desire to please you does in fact please you. And I hope I have that desire in all that I am doing. . . ."

Reading his journals, you see evidence of how even someone as spiritually focused as Merton could be distracted. In one passage he mentions staring at the pattern of lariats and cowboys on a visitor's shirt during worship, his mind wandering. If Merton could get distracted like that, so could I. Just because you're trying to be otherworldly doesn't mean that the worldly won't slip right into your head. Don't fight it. Listen to it. Pray your way through it.

"Praise the Lord from the earth," goes the psalm, "fire, and hail, snow, and vapors, stormy wind fulfilling his word, mountains, and all hills, fruitful trees, and all cedars, beasts, and all cattle, creeping things, and flying fowl" (Psalm 148:7–10, KJV). You praise God for everything you see and hear, everything on your wavelength. Andy barking, horns honking, the timer buzzing, the phone ringing, the hamster on his squeaking wheel, the kids giggling, praise the Lord.

The end of grace came with the single line that Dad repeated night after night: "Bless this food to our use, us to your service, and bless the hands that prepared it." There was the blessing.

"Amen," Dad finally said. "Amen," we responded. Mom went off to rescue her browning rolls, the mac-and-cheese made the rounds from the cork trivet, we asked Dad about what he heard on the news. Soon dinner would dissolve into a three-ring circus. We got up from the table to demonstrate some exercise we'd learned in phys ed. Diane did a somersault on the lime-green indoor-outdoor carpeting. Howard did a handstand and then showed us how many push-ups he could do. "Not on a full stomach," Mom exclaimed.

If we failed to appreciate the tomatoes in the salad, Mom would remind us, "These tomatoes cost nineteen cents a pound," as though that would add to our pleasure. If we wondered why we were getting an unfamiliar brand of cookies or brown-and-serve rolls, she would say sheepishly, "They were on sale," a holy refrain in a family with four growing children.

Our manners deteriorated. We made a boarding-house reach across the table, grabbing the butter. "No, no, no," Mom said, tapping the back of a hand with the back of her knife. Dad would go into a lecture on etiquette. "When I was in submarine corps during the war," he began, "some of the fellows told me I should give up on 'please' and 'thank you' and 'please pass the rolls.' Well, I told them I wasn't planning on spending my life on a submarine. I would say please..."

We hardly listened. We were in a rush. If there was any light left after dinner we would go back outside for a game of kick the can or freeze tag. There would be baths to take, books to read, bedtime. Still we'd had this quiet moment together when Dad asked God to bless our food and to bless us.

◆ ◆ ◆

The idea of blessing anything is not that common today. It means stopping and slowing down. We usually like to jump in and do something. We want the car to start right away, we want the computer to be ready to go, we hate delays when we get on the Internet. We want dinner now. But blessing is as ancient as faith and central to it. What did Jesus do before he fed the five thousand? He blessed the bread and broke it. What did he do when all the disciples were gathered in the Upper Room for the Last Supper? "Jesus took bread and blessed it and broke it and gave it to them, saying, 'Take, eat; this is my body.' And he took the cup and when he had given thanks, he gave it to them, and they all drank of it."

This was the opposite of fast food. A nutritionist I know makes the point that saying grace is good for the digestion. It gives us a chance to slow down before we eat. We smell the casserole cooling or the steak waiting to be cut, the gastric juices get going but we don't start shoveling in immediately. "Bless this food to our use" could be a prescription on the back of the bag of groceries. Thankfulness at the dinner table is good for the body *and* soul. You certainly enjoy your food more when you season it with gratitude. You've thanked God and the cook.

Getting dinner on the table is a nightly miracle and in families it's so easy to forget the miracle makers or even to acknowledge them, especially if they do their duties well and effortlessly. Efficiency can make the work dangerously invisible. I was a newlywed when I worked on a story from a writer who was listing the reasons for her fifty years of happy marriage. "Tommy has never once forgotten to thank me for a dinner I've cooked," she wrote.

Note to self: thank your wife for dinner. Be like Dad blessing Mom.

We are not wholly responsible for the food on our table. Not only are there the "hands that prepared it," but also the farmers who toiled, the rains that watered, the soil that nurtured, the sunshine that blessed and all that help we got to earn the money we spent at the supermarket. The self-made man is a fiction, the luck we credit for our good fortune an illusion. Thankfulness reminds us of that. Even the most rudimentary grace has the essential ingredient of gratitude, whether it's the standard "God is great, God is good. Let us be thankful for our food" or the summer camp classic, "Rub-a-dub-dub. Thanks for the grub. Yeah, God!"

Asking for a blessing means acknowledging that someone has power over you or can give you something you want. Now it's just a courtesy to ask your future in-laws for their blessing on your marriage, but there was a time when it was a make-or-break conversation. When a minister or priest blesses the congregation it's a reminder that God is the great source of our well-being: "May the Lord bless you and keep you. May the Lord make his countenance shine upon you and be gracious to you. May the Lord turn his countenance to you and grant you peace."

In the Bible, Esau, the firstborn, came in from the fields so hungry that he sold his birthright to his younger twin brother, Jacob, for a bowl of lentil stew. (My wife, Carol, likes to remind me of this every time she serves up her lentil stew.) When Esau was away, Jacob fooled his blind father Isaac by pretending to be Esau. At his mother's urging, he dressed in his brother's rough clothes so that he would smell like Esau and put goat hair on his arms so he would be hairy like Esau. (As a kid in Sunday school I thought that Isaac must have been pretty dense to mistake a furry hide for a hairy forearm.) The ruse worked and Jacob won his father's blessing: "May God give you showers from the sky, olive oil from the earth, plenty of grain and new wine. May the nations serve you, may peoples bow down to you... Those who curse you will be cursed, and those who bless you will be blessed" (Genesis 27:28–29, CEB).

Enigmatic and deceptive as it is, the blessing holds. Jacob becomes the patriarch of a new nation after wrestling with the angel who changes his name to Israel. I think the longing for a parent's blessing is just as deep and hard-wired in us today, even if we might not use that word. To hear your father bless you night after night is bound to have its effect. Sometimes I wonder why I was never tarred with the brush that turns religion into a dark thing and God into the big scary Father in heaven ready to condemn us for our least faults. If I knew that God loved me, it wasn't just because I was told so — and I was, countless times — but also because I experienced the love of God through Dad's prayers.

Monasteries observe the offices of the day, praying at specific times. "Seven times a day I praise you for your righteous laws," says the psalmist in Psalm 119:164 (NIV). Making grace a habit keeps prayer on the agenda.

◆ ◆ ◆

As brave as I am in writing about prayer, it's taken me years to be brave about saying grace in public. In a New York restaurant where there are waiters hovering, ready to sprinkle some parmesan cheese on your pasta or grind some fresh pepper, I won't ask my friends or colleagues to bow their heads before we dig in. When I'm with some holy person in a clerical collar I've learned to pause before lifting my fork. "Is he going to say grace?" I wonder. Will we be like that grandmother and kid in the Norman Rockwell painting who are praying to the rest of the diners' bemusement? I'm self-conscious. Are all eyes on us, the only two people praying in this restaurant?

I've decided it really doesn't matter. First of all, it's magnificently self-centered to think that anybody else is looking at me in a restaurant filled with people who all have their own concerns. Second, self-consciousness is often a prelude to prayer. "Who am I to pray this? Why would God be interested?" you wonder and then you jump in. Faith often requires an attitude of "I can't believe I'm doing this but I'm going to do it anyway." Be bold. Mighty forces will come to your aid.

At home when we have friends for dinner, I have fewer qualms. I used to wonder, "Should I say grace if they're not believers?" Will they find it awkward? Will they be bored? I've given up that too. Let them see this as my little eccentricity, like people who collect paperweights or make their dogs do tricks at the table. I say grace at dinner. Who am I to guess what they believe or don't believe? They won't mind. I might go a little faster when guests are here or give them a signal so they don't eat half their salad before I've bowed my head, but grace is what we do. It's the habit of the house.

Carol and I started saying grace at home when our two boys were young, the apple falling not far from the tree. I couldn't then and I still can't extemporize a grace as sweet as the ones I heard in my childhood. As the boys grew older, I asked them to participate. We went around the table, each of us in charge for a night, Carol, Tim,

Will, me, then back to Carol. If you want to know what's on your children's minds, ask them to say grace.

Like my father, I could see all those reasons for gratitude.

I remember pausing outside our apartment and looking in one winter night when the boys were young. Carol was boiling water for spaghetti, the steam already fogging up the windows. William was sitting at the kitchen table, writing in a school workbook, his hand curled around his pencil, his mouth forming a word. Timothy was dashing in from the living room, the tuft of his milkweed hair moving across the bottom of the windows like a duck in a shooting gallery. The light was on above the piano and Carol was reaching in the cabinet for the box of pasta. She wouldn't pour it in until she saw the whites of my eyes.

At once I could see my life from the outside, how fortunate I was, how blessed. Soon I'd be on the inside. A kiss to Carol, put away the briefcase, hug the boys, settle any fraternal disputes. It was always a race. Could we get it all done? Set the table, eat dinner, wash the dishes, read to both boys before bed, hear their prayers, get them to sleep, talk to Carol, pay the bills, get to sleep ourselves. There was hardly a moment. But this. I could see my life from a different view, as others might have seen it, maybe as God saw it. I was the luckiest guy on earth.

It made me understand why Dad would sometimes pause during grace, overwhelmed by emotion. If only we could see how beautiful our lives are. If only we could just reflect on the day. Dad was the weeper in the family. He had what my wife would call "the gift of tears," a trait that has been passed along to my older son, Will.

Let me not gloss over Dad's outbursts of anger, but when they occurred at the dinner table we usually found something funny in it. When he threw his fork down after a bite of Mom's chicken broccoli casserole with a risky teaspoon of curry in it, he barked, "Who put that India stuff in here?" Mom said meekly, "I wanted to try something different." We giggled, then laughed till tears rolled down our cheeks. Even Dad laughed.

I once provoked Howard into throwing a fork at me—the argument was about Bill Cosby, if you must know. I cried. Then someone pointed out how funny it was, and we laughed. Even Dad got his chances back. He could come up with a one-liner that put us in stitches. In old age, he moved mighty slow, his joints aching from arthritis, his back bent over from spinal stenosis, his feet in their clunky lace-less white sneakers. He followed several steps behind our energetic tennis-playing mom.

"I just pray and pray for patience," Mom said.

"That's one prayer God hasn't answered yet," Dad muttered from his walker.

We laughed then and we laughed again when Howard retold that story at Dad's memorial service. Everybody in the packed church laughed. Mom laughed from the front pew. Laughter is as healing as gratitude, maybe even more so.

When I hear Paul's extraordinary statement in Romans 8:38–39— "For I am persuaded that neither death, nor life, nor angels, nor principalities, nor powers, nor things present, nor things to come, nor height, nor depth, nor any other creature, shall be able to separate us from the love of God which is in Christ Jesus our Lord"—I think of my family. It's the feeling of safety and security that I grew up with. It's the satisfying love I find at my own dinner table when I say grace with my wife and my children. Here is love. Nothing can separate me from it.

Dad's graces continued through his mid-eighties. Wracked with pain, he got to a point where the only place he was comfortable was lying in bed. The neuropathy in his feet made walking downstairs for breakfast a trial. Still, whenever the family got together for dinner or even if it was just him and Mom in the breakfast room, he said grace. The words came haltingly, the thoughts were briefer. There was little of the six o'clock news but more of us, our spouses, his nine grandchildren. He always ended by saying, "Bless this food to our use, us to your service, and bless the hands that prepared it."

Mom and her much-blessed hands took magnificent care of him until the day he simply couldn't get out of bed. He spent the last five months of his life in a nursing facility on the lush grounds of a home for retired Presbyterian ministers that took in local residents when they had an empty bed. He flirted with his nurses and befriended his roommate. We pushed him in his wheelchair through the gardens of oaks, palms, roses, citrus trees, birds of paradise. He was confused sometimes and he slept for hours, but he wasn't unhappy.

I flew out to visit every month. Once, our younger son, Timothy, and I drove straight from the airport to his bedside. "We just flew in, Dad," I said.

"From Puerto Rico?" he asked.

"No, Dad, from New York," I said.

"Close enough," he responded, as though it was a nice joke. Why should he have to bother with such geographic details when he was on a larger cosmic journey?

I remember thinking we should have some big profound conversation about the end of things. Perhaps he would want to pass on some advice or share some memory of his childhood. He didn't. We would sit in the sun by his old convertible that I drove on my visits and he would point to a passing truck or admire the statue of Jesus in one corner of the garden. The last time I saw him still conscious, I kissed him good-bye on his forehead, the same place he kissed me as a boy after my bedtime prayers. "I love you, Dad," I said.

"Tell your wife," he said, the cylinders in his brain moving slowing, searching for the right words. "Tell your wife," he said, "that I am loved."

He was loved. That much we knew.

Less than a month later my sister Gioia had the last conversation anybody had with him. He was in hospice care and too weak now to go on wheelchair jaunts. He didn't move from his bed. "Dad," she said, teary-eyed, "I'm going to miss you so much."

He looked up at her and asked, "Am I moving?"

Yes, sort of.

He slipped into a coma or some state of minimal awareness and I flew out to see him for the last time.

We sat by his bed for five days while he slowly left us, his vitals winding down, his hands getting colder, his feet getting bluer. He could squeeze hands, but then his hand became weaker. He had no water, no food, no nourishment. Every day we thought would be his last, but he rallied when we appeared, his four children, our spouses, his grandchildren, their spouses, talking around him and above him like we did at dinner. He waited until four in the morning, when none of us were present, to die. Never the first to leave a party, he wouldn't go when we were still there.

We all spoke at the funeral, each of us wearing one of his bowties (the girls wore them on their wrists). Gioia talked about following in Dad's footsteps in her career, becoming a professional fundraiser and non-profit executive like him. Diane described his generosity of character and his tireless volunteer work. Her husband, Mike, spoke of his submarine service, three war patrols in the Pacific during World War II. Our son Will confessed that when he was eleven and his fifth-grade teacher asked the class what their goals were, Will said that he wanted to have four children and nine grandchildren, just like his grandfather. I sang a song that Dad loved and then reminded the packed church how he had prayed for all of them. "I'll hold a good thought for you" was how he put it.

But Howard got it just right, Howard who had sat holding his hand at his bedside, hardly letting go. "When I was sitting with Dad these last few days," he said, "I tried to think if there were any things that I needed to talk about. Were there any things I still needed to say?

"All I could come up with was thanks. You see, Dad let me be me. That's what he gave all of us. He let us be ourselves. He encouraged us to do just what we wanted."

I don't know what comes to people's minds when they say, "We were blessed." But what comes to my mind is a childhood when Dad prayed for us night after night at the dinner table. Such prayers must be called grace because they offer a heaping serving of God's grace. We were blessed by them, richly blessed.

## CHAPTER TWO

# Prayer as Conversation

*"Hi, God."*

Our church youth group was putting on the worship service for Sunday. I was picked to lead the congregation in prayer. At age fourteen I'd sat through plenty of prayers led by one of our robed ministers, solemn, stately, dignified. But I wanted to do something different. What was the most honest thing I could say about prayer? How would I address God if nobody else were there?

I walked to the lectern clutching my notes, my bellbottoms that I'd already grown out of billowing above my skinny ankles, my hair an unruly mess. "Let us pray," I said. The congregation bowed their heads. I took a deep breath, looked down at the words I'd scribbled with a ballpoint pen and went to the top of all my polished phrases. "Hi, God," I said as boldly as I could into the microphone. Not "Dear Heavenly Father" or "Dear Lord" but "Hi, God," because it seemed like the best way to open this conversation. "Hi, God," because that was the way you'd start a frank conversation with anyone you loved.

Prayer is conversation. It's a conversation you can have all day. It's a conversation that has gone on for most of my life—give or take a few years of the silent treatment on my part. Bob Hostetler, who has a terrific blog on prayer, suggests in his book with the winsome title *Quit Going to Church* that it could be just sitting in a chair with a cup of coffee the first part of the morning. "You might tell him about your hopes and plans and fears and worries for the day or you might ask him to tell you his.... The important thing is not so much the words you use as the habit you pursue."

That's it. Make it a habit. If I could only pass on one piece of advice about prayer, this would be it: Pick a time and place for prayer and try to do it every day.

Don't be too ambitious about how much time you devote to it. Better to take on a challenge that's manageable than one that's going to overwhelm you and frustrate you until you finally give up. If it's only going to be five minutes, then five minutes it is. Perfect. Five minutes of quiet with just you and your prayers and God listening, or you listening to God, is impressive. If you can do that, congratulate yourself. It's an accomplishment you should be proud of. You've made a place for God in your life. You will reap the benefits.

Whenever experts talk about New Year's resolutions, they always stress that you should give yourself an achievable goal. Working out at the gym for an hour and a half five days a week is not going to hold if you've barely set foot in the place in the last year. Do something small. Better that it can grow into something bigger than you slacking off and giving up altogether.

My insistence on a particular place for prayer might surprise you. Can't you pray anywhere? Isn't God everywhere? "If I take the wings of the morning," the psalmist says, "and dwell in the uttermost parts of the sea, even there thy hand shall lead me and thy right hand shall guide me" (Psalm 139:9, KJV). Yes, God is everywhere. But the external stimuli of a familiar place are going to help you connect. Familiarity does not breed contempt in the spiritual life. Familiarity makes it all the easier. You're here for a regular conversation, "Hi, God." You don't want to be thinking about the furniture or what color the drapes are. The background should be so comfortable that you don't even have to pay attention to where you are.

There are a thousand ways to pray in the middle of a busy day. You'll say something quietly to yourself, you'll hold the lyrics to a song in your head, you'll scroll a picture of calm and comfort through your brain when you're feeling anything but calm. You'll take a few deep breaths and remind yourself of God's love. You'll sing along with the car radio. You'll stretch your hands, releasing tension. You'll flex your toes. You'll read a passage of Scripture on Facebook. In your imagination you'll zap someone with God's love across the conference table at a particularly rancorous meeting. You'll smile. You'll laugh. You'll thank someone for something they did that they thought no one noticed. You'll praise a colleague or a cashier or the janitor at your kids' school. You'll tell a friend how much you care about them. You'll buy an "I'm thinking of you" card and mail it. You'll send a quick e-mail to a troubled soul, reminding her that she is in your prayers.

If you give yourself some concentrated, uninterrupted, dedicated time of prayer every day, all those other ways of praying will come easier. It's the unpolluted aquifer that will feed your best intentions. It will give you perspective on the whole day.

A couple of years ago my brother Howard sent me an e-mail with one of those two-megabyte attachments that make you wonder what you're going to have to scroll through. This turned out to be a picture of a beautiful Alpine meadow, yellow flowers in green grass beneath a cerulean sky, a brooding black helicopter in the background. "We flew here for lunch," he wrote, "only twenty minutes from home."

Howard and his wife, Julie, are helicopter pilots, among other talents, and their helicopter, when it's not being rented by the local police department, sits in the airport near their home in the middle of a dense, smoggy megalopolis of jammed freeways. All they had to do was lift off and fly to the mountains to get this view. *Flee like a bird to your mountain.*

"Just the sort of trip I look for in prayer," I wrote my more skeptical brother. To lift off, be airborne, look down on my troubles as they shrink into proper size, and take myself to a mental meadow.

My prayer habit is sustained by my morning commute on the New York City subway. My mind is freshest in the morning, my need to set my thinking right is also great. Not for nothing did the psalmist say, "My voice shalt thou hear in the morning, O Lord; in the morning will I direct my prayer unto thee, and will look up" (Psalm 5:3, KJV). If I have scanned the news at breakfast, I can be in an ornery mood. As I've said, there is always a story to get me riled up or irritated.

Anything bad about the economy is sure to convince me that I'm headed for the poorhouse. The fear rattling my confidence is reason enough to pray.

I take the elevator down to the subway platform and wait for a train. I often run into some neighbor but we all have our morning habits. We want to be in different cars on the train, we stand at different spots on the platform. Most of my pals know that I use my commute for prayer and meditation. But they're taking out newspapers, Kindles, iPads, paperbacks or documents they've downloaded onto their phones. My Jewish brethren are reading Scripture in Hebrew; there's always a Hispanic neighbor studying the *Santa Biblia*.

We live in the upper reaches of Manhattan near the end of the A train. I'm usually lucky enough to get a seat. I have two old battered, dog-eared copies of the New Testament and Psalms printed by the Gideons International. One was actually picked up on a subway seat and has someone else's underlining and scribbling, the pentimento of its previous ownership. Both copies have been taped at the spine. I keep one in my gym bag, one in my briefcase so I'm never without it. I used to be able to read the small type without glasses. No more. When my neighbors see me take out my Bible it's a sign that I have something else in mind for my commute rather than chatting. Some of them must think, "Yikes, a Jesus freak. I sure hope he *doesn't* talk to me."

Several years ago the *New York Times* was doing a story on prayer and after the reporter interviewed me they sent a photographer to take a picture of me praying on the subway. "I'm sorry," I said, "you can't do that. If I know a photographer is taking a picture of me I won't be praying. I'll be too self-conscious. I'll be faking it." We settled on a compromise. The photographer would take a picture of me reading my little green Bible. Then he would get off at the 125th Street station and I could pray then.

The subway has become such a natural place for me to pray that I sometimes fear if I don't have a morning commute, I'll still put myself on a train just to pray. It's my meditation chapel, my Chartres. All the external stimuli tell me it's time to pray. The white noise of the wheels rumbling along the tracks, the squeak of the brakes at each station, the jostling movement of the train, the opening and closing of the doors, the sound of the people shifting around me, the conductor's voice. "Watch the closing doors, please," could be my prayer call.

Choose a place to pray and you anoint what's around you to help you in your spiritual journey. You make it holy in the most mundane way. Sleep experts will tell people who suffer from insomnia to use their beds just for sleeping—not eating, catching up on work, watching TV. You want your bed to trigger all your impulses to relax and fall asleep. When I go to my office and sit at my desk I'm stimulated to work. When I click on my computer I'm ready to sort through a million e-mails. When I sink into the sofa in front of the TV I'm ready to be entertained. When I get onto the subway train in the morning I'm ready to pray.

I usually read a psalm or some fragment of Scripture before I close my eyes. It helps me concentrate, but I don't insist on it. Some days I'm ready to close my eyes the minute the train pulls out of the station.

For any novice in prayer I must immediately defuse any misconceptions you hold about this plunge into the otherworldly, this reach for the divine. When I'm praying there is no celestial buzz about my head, no flutter of angel wings. I don't go into a trance. I'm not on a magic carpet ride. Prayer is not an escape. That's what you get from drugs and alcohol, or at least that's their short-lived promise. In the words of Sister Joan Chittister, "Prayer enables us to be immersed in what is fundamentally and truly divine in life right now. It is not meant to be a bridge to somewhere else because God is not somewhere else. God is here."

God is here. Go meet him.

"Aren't you afraid you'll miss your station?" someone once asked me. Of course not. You're always aware of what's going on around you. At times I find myself leaning into the world around me. Other times I lean away from it. The external noise can keep me focused or become part of my meandering: "125th Street," the conductor can say, "next stop 59th Street." That's a reminder of a long uninterrupted stretch underground before I need to change trains, an alert to make the most of this time.

Some writers talk about the discipline of meditation and prayer as though you have to take a mental whip to the thoughts that swirl around in your head and corral them back to your intention. You're supposed to seek a sublime emptiness to find the presence of God. In all my years of praying I've never been very successful at that. The brain is too active (at least mine is). Instead I think you should be very forgiving about all the thoughts that enter your head when you pray.

They are not just distractions. They might be the main event. This is what you came for, to hear what's happening in your head. Listen to it. Pay attention. Ask God where you need help. Drop your worries in God's lap. Look for where you are needed.

When you say "Hi, God," God can say "Hi" back in the most startling ways. It could be when you're praying, but it might be when you're driving home from work, standing in line at the supermarket or watching TV at the end of a long day.

Back in the late 1980s a Massachusetts couple was watching a made-for-TV movie called *God Bless the Child*. Mare Winningham played a single mom who lost her job and her apartment. She and her daughter ended up sleeping on cots in homeless shelters. A social worker finds them a house, but things go from bad to worse. The daughter gets seriously ill and the mom feels she has to put the girl up for adoption so she can get the care she needs.

James and Terry Orcutt had been asking themselves if there was something more they could do for God. They'd raised their kids, they both had decent jobs, they were living in a small rented house. As the credits of *God Bless the Child* rolled across the screen, tears ran down Terry's face. James almost jumped out of his recliner galvanized, as though someone had grabbed him by the shoulders and shaken him. "All that woman needed was a room like one of ours," Terry said, "until she could get back on her feet."

The Orcutts had flipped on the TV to unwind before bed. Now they stayed up until 2:00 AM talking. What could they do? They couldn't take in the homeless in their house; their landlord would never accept that. But maybe they could help out in other ways. What if they collected food, clothes, furniture, money to pay an electric bill, to give to people who were in desperate straits? Their grown son's bedroom had a bed and dresser in it that they could easily give away. "God," they prayed, "we'll do whatever it takes."

The next night they drew "We Collect for People in Need" signs and posted them around town. In a matter of days their basement was filled with chairs, sofas, bedding, food, plates, silverware, pots, microwaves. Others wanted to help too. James opened up the yellow pages and called up homeless shelters and halfway houses. Then he loaded up his car, a Chevy Cavalier with 120,000 miles on it. He borrowed a roof rack, and he and Terry started to make deliveries. They'd carry a sofa up two flights of stairs to a mom and two kids who had only one small mattress. They'd deliver a mini-fridge to a man whose only source of power was an extension cord strung from an upstairs neighbor's apartment. They made sure his bill was paid so that his power could be turned back on.

At one moment James wondered if they were being too soft and unsophisticated. "Should we ask people to fill out anything to show they're qualified?" he asked Terry.

Terry shook her head. "In all my readings of the Bible," she said, "I don't believe there's one time when Jesus ever asked if a person was worth helping."

They started an organization called My Brother's Keeper. They would accept donations to cover expenses but they wouldn't ask anything from the government. The government *would* want paperwork and that's not who they were. When someone asks where the furniture and supplies come from, they're given a small wooden cross. My Brother's Keeper now has a fleet of trucks and a 15,000-square-foot warehouse. They've helped tens of thousands of families.

The Orcutts prayed regularly. "Hi, God" was a habit with a question at the end: "What else can we do?" It's like that question you ask someone going through a crisis, an illness, a death in the family: "Is there anything I can do?" James and Terry were pretty insistent about it, repetition in prayer being a good thing. But the answer didn't come when they had their heads bowed or were on their knees. It came when they were watching a made-for-TV movie.

If you listened to my head in prayer, you'd be surprised at the racket going on in there. None of it is going to sound that holy. I'm irritable, I complain, I replay conversations at work and e-mails I sent. I self-justify and talk nonsense. I obsess about my health and my appearance. Prayer is reaching for God. Be suspicious of anyone who promises you heaven each time you're out of the gate. More often you'll be mentally balancing the checkbook and wondering when the adjustable-rate mortgage is going to bounce back up. Take it as a chance to ask God to help you trust him with your finances.

"Hi, God," I'll say, "it's me, Rick. Remember all that stuff I told you about yesterday and what I was really worried about? Well, today, something else just hit me..." If God seems silent, does it really mean he's not listening? The best moments with the people you love can be filled with silence. Think of the down time you spend with a spouse. You're both puttering around the house. One of you is reading a book, the other is washing the dishes or wiping the table after dinner. The kids are watching TV. Neither of you says anything but you feel each other's presence. One of the greatest pleasures of marriage is being with someone and not having to speak. God time is like that. It offers the gift of companionable silence.

Some days on the subway, when I'm ready to close my eyes and pray, somebody will sit down next to me and I'll know I need to talk. "Hi, Rick. How are you?" says a neighbor I haven't seen for a long time. I sigh. *Don't you see my Bible in my lap? Can't you tell I'm busy?* What arrogance! Maybe the thing God had in mind for me that morning was to listen to what my neighbor had to say.

One June morning it was a guy I hadn't seen much since our boys played Little League together. He's a high school teacher and was a terrific coach for our boys. I loved hanging out with him, but I wasn't in a chatty mood just now. "Hi, Rick," he said. "Hi, Bob," I said, "how are you?" I reluctantly slid my Bible back into my gym bag.

"I'm doing okay," he said. We talked about our boys first, where they were, what they were doing. Small talk. But then he said, "I'm heading downtown to hand in my resignation. This is my last year of teaching."

"Wow," I said. "What are you going to do next?"

He talked about some of his plans and how he was feeling in the lurch, untethered, uncertain exactly what the future would hold. He seemed glad to share this milestone with someone, his last official day as a public schoolteacher. By the time I got off the subway I knew that conversation was more important than any of the prayer chitchat that would have taken place. "Hi, God," you say, and God comes in the form of a friend who needs to talk. *Just as you did it to one of the least of these you did it to me.*

Another morning I was meditating on a verse from the Psalms (30:5, KJV), trying to remember what I'd read ("Weeping may endure for a night, but joy comes in the morning"). From the other end of the train I heard the strident voice of a West Indian woman I think of as the A-train evangelist. "READ THE BIBLE," she said. "Listen to the message of the Bible and be saved. God wants you to read the Bible. Hear God's word."

I sighed. *She's so loud. I didn't want loud this morning. I want peace and quiet. I wish she'd go back the other direction.* She meandered through the crowded subway train, chanting at top volume. Still with my eyes closed, I could hear people stepping aside to make room for her. I could imagine none of them were making eye contact or taking any of her tracts. "I wish she'd shut up," someone muttered. I echoed the thought. What a holy, kindly, forgiving soul I am!

Then just as she came to my end of the car, she started reading a psalm from her Bible. "Weeping may endure for a night, but joy comes in the morning," she proclaimed, just the passage I'd been saying to myself. So much for the word of God transforming me. I opened my eyes, looked at her and smiled. I stood up to get off the train. "Thanks," I said. "That's one of my favorite psalms too."

"READ THE BIBLE," she said.

◆ ◆ ◆

How do you know if God's talking to you in this conversation you've started? How do you know he's saying something back to your "Hi, God"?

Here's a bit of wisdom I got from job-hunting expert Richard Bolles. "The Holy Spirit is the Lord of our time," he said to me when I was interviewing him for a *Guideposts* story. He is the author of the book *What Color Is Your Parachute?* a perennial bestseller and an essential text for anyone looking for a job or changing careers. Bolles also happens to be an Episcopal priest and in fact wrote the book after going through his own career change from parish ministry to a different way of helping people.

We met in Washington, DC, on a luminous April day. I had listened to him give a talk to a group of priests in the shadow of the National Cathedral, and then we drove to the cherry trees out by the Jefferson Memorial. Sitting under the trees as they were dripping blossoms while a surprising number of Japanese tourists swirled around us taking pictures, we talked about time management. We were discussing how in an office there were always interruptions to whatever you hoped to get done. I was telling him how I tried to give myself goals each day but rarely accomplished all that I set out to do. Something was always coming up. A phone call, a last-minute meeting, a demand for a new article, a request for a rewrite of a story that I'd already rewritten two times, a conversation with a colleague, a book landing on my desk, unexpected news from home. There were days I wanted to throw up my hands in frustration.

"Think of all those interruptions as coming from the Holy Spirit," he said. "Instead of trying to control time, be open to what time is offering you." And then he gave me that phrase: "The Holy Spirit is the Lord of our time." It wasn't at all the subject of the article I wrote, but it's what I remember most from that interview. I say it to myself all the time, especially when I don't think I'm getting anywhere. *The Holy Spirit is the Lord of our time.*

Be open to what the Holy Spirit is saying. Pay attention to the nudges that come. If a colleague wants to talk about her frustrations raising her teenage son or has chosen this moment to reveal some deeply held insecurity, it is not a moment to stick to the schedule. Listen. A golden opportunity has come your way. You are being asked to do something important. Instead of choosing someone else, God has chosen you. You in all your own insecurities and uncertainties, you in your ham-fisted attempts at kindness, are being given a chance. This is a tremendous benefit of prayer. To make us aware of how we can serve. To give us the courage and the insight to know when we should drop everything and help someone else. Over the long haul, the goals on the schedules that we give ourselves get met, especially if they're entrusted to a higher power. The torturing, niggling anxieties shrink to a manageable size when the big needs have been addressed.

Take a moment to say "Hi, God" and you can get something that you didn't even know you were looking for.

Emily Procter is a beautiful LA actress, known for her role as Detective Calleigh Duquesne on the long-running TV show *CSI: Miami*. Before she was famous, before she landed the part that gave her financial security and an enviable measure of stardom, she was just another aspiring Hollywood actress going from audition to audition. Each lucky break was supposed to lead to another, a supporting role here, a sitcom there, a drama in the works, the chance to make a valuable contact. But as she was making her way in a brutally tough market, she found herself becoming too self-absorbed. Had she lost enough weight? Did her hair look right? Was there a reason she hadn't gotten called back after that last audition?

Just to get out of herself she volunteered at the soup kitchen at the church a couple of blocks from her apartment. Every Monday in her very unglamorous green overalls and clogs, she'd serve the homeless and the hungry and those who were just down on their luck. Her father was a doctor back in North Carolina. Her mom volunteered with AIDS patients. She was used to signing up for service projects at her church back home. What to do with herself while waiting for that big break? This soup kitchen was where prayer led her.

For most of us—and I'm including myself—that would be the end of it. Emily would volunteer at the church every Monday until Mondays became too busy. It's easy serving the homeless in an institutional setting. It's safer to relate to a needy person when you are simply dishing out lasagna and salad.

But there was one homeless guy in a wheelchair on Wilshire Boulevard who never came to the soup kitchen. He sat in his shorts and red windbreaker reading. One December Monday, as Emily was heading to the church in her green overalls, she stopped and asked him, "I work at the soup kitchen at All Saints. Want to come with me and get lunch?"

"Yeah!" the guy said.

"I'm Emily," she said.

"I'm Jim," he said.

She grabbed his wheelchair and started pushing but couldn't maneuver it very well in her clunky shoes. Finally she had to tell Jim that she couldn't do it in her clogs. "I'm going home for Christmas," she said, "but I'll be back the first Monday after New Year's. We'll have lunch then."

"Okay," Jim said. He probably didn't believe her. Who would? But true to her word, Emily Procter showed up the Monday after New Year's in tennis shoes and whisked Jim off to the All Saints soup kitchen.

It became a ritual with her, and the best of spiritual growth comes through such rituals. Every Monday Emily pushed Jim in his wheelchair to the soup kitchen. It was a relief to talk to somebody who wasn't in show business, who wasn't bragging about what part she had been offered or what movie she hoped to be cast in. It was good to know Jim. One day three months after they'd met—this was the part of the story my mom loved the most—Jim took Emily's hand and pressed some money in it. Forty dollars. A lot for a guy who lived on the streets.

"Jim, what's this for?" she asked.

"I want to tell you something," he said very solemnly. "I think you're very pretty, but you really need to buy a new outfit. I saved up this money."

Emily realized that he had never seen her in anything but her grungy green overalls. "Thanks, Jim," she said. "I guess I've never told you: I'm an actress. I have lots of other clothes." They laughed about that.

Jim remained a good friend of Emily's for years and still is. They ate breakfast at a coffee shop. She helped him get a place to live in affordable housing. He'd been a terrible alcoholic and almost died before he got sober, he told her. "God stood by me even when I wasn't standing by me," he said. Jim was the voice of reason Emily needed when she feared she was getting too wrapped up in her career. He gave her perspective on life, a larger view. He was an answer to prayer, the friend she didn't know she needed until she found him.

There's another story of an actress who paid attention to the meandering of her prayers. Marcia Gay Harden played one of her best parts for an audience of one. Marcia is probably best known for her Oscar-winning role as Lee Krasner, the artist Jackson Pollock's wife, but she's been in a ton of movies and plays. I first heard about her from my friend and prayer partner Arthur Caliandro (for more about the prayer help I got from him, see chapter eight). He was for many years the senior minister at Marble Collegiate Church on Fifth Avenue, not far from the Guideposts office. Marcia was a member of the congregation, and as Arthur said, "She's got a terrific story."

In her early days as an actress, she lived in DC, doing a lot of theater and supporting herself as a waitress. Someday she hoped to work full-time as an actress, get her Screen Actors Guild card to do TV and movies and move to New York, but for now, this was it. One day two women came into the restaurant where she worked, sat down in her section and told her they recognized her from a play she'd been in. They had a special part to offer her, not on stage but at the Georgetown University Hospital. They were from the Make-A-Wish Foundation, which grants wishes to terminally ill children.

"A seven-year-old girl named Bonnie is dying of cancer," they told her. "She doesn't have much more than a month to live. *Snow White* is her favorite movie and Bonnie's wish is to meet Snow White. Could you be Snow White?"

Marcia didn't hesitate. How could she? She promised she'd be available to play Snow White whenever she was needed.

The trouble was, the day that the Make-A-Wish Foundation settled on was the day she had a casting call to be in an Oliver Stone film. It was the only day Oliver Stone would be in DC casting for his movie, an opportunity a budding actress like Marcia couldn't afford to miss. The casting director didn't need to stress how important it was. "Whatever conflicts you have, reschedule them."

Marcia called the Make-A-Wish ladies. "Couldn't you make it another day?"

"I'm sorry," she was told. "Bonnie's running out of time."

A promise was a promise, especially a promise to make a sick little girl's wish come true. It was one of those "Hi, God" moments when you've prayed to do the right thing and the right thing feels like it's all wrong. Marcia feared she was making the worst career mistake of her life, but she forced herself to say no to the casting call. She immersed herself in the role of Snow White. She found a good costume, reread the story, watched the Disney movie and could rattle off the names of the seven dwarfs backwards and forwards. She had the part down cold.

Still, the morning of the performance she was full of doubts about the choice she'd made. She drove to the hospital in Georgetown in her yellow VW dressed in her Snow White costume, wiping the tears from her eyes. She made one last call from a pay phone to the casting director to beg for a chance to reschedule. "No, Marcia," she was told. "This is it."

She was running late. This *was* it. She wiped away her tears, then asked for directions at the hospital's reception desk. She dashed down a hall and found Bonnie's mother and sister standing outside the girl's room. They gave her some presents to give to Bonnie. Marcia took a deep breath and went inside. A small, painfully thin girl looking much younger than her years was sitting on a pallet on the floor. Her pale face lit up. "Snow White!" she said. All of Marcia's doubts vanished.

"Hello, Bonnie," she said. "I'm so glad to see you. I'm so sorry Grumpy, Sneezy, Sleepy, Doc, Bashful, Happy and Dopey weren't able to make it."

They talked for a while about the handsome prince and Marcia gave her the presents. Then Bonnie took Marcia's hand and asked the toughest question of all: "When I die, will the prince kiss me and then I'll wake up again?"

What could Marcia say? How could you answer a child's question like that? She closed her eyes for a second and tried to imagine how

Bonnie was feeling, how lonely it must be to be this young and this sick. She'd always felt there was an inherent mystery to acting, that when she found a role she connected with—a role she was meant to play—it felt like God was using her for something good. This was such a moment, as though everything she did was a prayer.

"No, Bonnie," she said, "it's even better. When you go to heaven, God will kiss you and then you'll wake up again."

Bonnie died a week later. Marcia eventually got her Screen Actors Guild card and moved to New York. She spent more years going to acting classes, waiting tables, living in crummy apartments before she got her big break and ultimately her Academy Award. But the role she played for a sick seven-year-old was one of the most important she had ever played.

◆ ◆ ◆

Would that all my prayers ended up with such noble results. I like to think I would have done the right thing like Marcia, but I don't know. The inner voice has to contend with tons of well-meant advice urging us to look out for number one, to go for the big chance, to do what we have to do to get ahead. "It's a nasty world out there and nobody's going to give you a prize for being unselfish," someone will say. Nice guys finish last. Look out for yourself because no one else is going to. Even my big-hearted dad had these grumpy, Eeyore-like, woe-is-me moments when he would mutter that he would have done better in life if he hadn't looked out for the other guy. "What am I supposed to do with that?" I would wonder. "How is that supposed to help me?" I'm glad Marcia could admit to her doubts. Up until the moment she stepped into Bonnie's hospital room she wasn't sure. How could she help? Was she doing what God wanted her to do? Only then was there clarity.

Prayer is a way of slogging through the inner conflicts, looking for the truth. It requires honesty. That's one reason I've called this section "Hi, God." A spontaneous conversation with God, one where you say what's really on your mind, is more likely to lead to a satisfying conclusion than anything you could have planned. Sure, you can give yourself a pep talk but when you're at your wit's end, spell it out to God. Say the worst. Expose yourself. Come clean. Just articulating it will help. Later you might even find yourself telling someone else just what you were telling God. It could be just the right person.

Susan Peabody was a single mom in Berkeley, California. Ever since her husband died, her teenage son Karl had become more and more withdrawn. She tried to talk to him, but the more she reached out, the more he pulled away. His junior year of high school, his report card revealed that he had been absent ninety-five times from classes and had six failing grades. She sent him to the school therapist, grounded him, pleaded with him. Nothing worked.

Finally she got down on her knees. She didn't mince words. "God, I can't do anything more for my son. I'm at the end of my rope. I'm giving the whole thing up to you."

She was at work when she got a phone call. A man introduced himself as the school guidance counselor. "I want to talk to you about

Karl's absences," he said. Before he could say another word, Susan choked up and all her frustration and sadness came pouring out.

"I love my son," she said, "but I just don't know what to do. I've tried everything to get Karl to go back to school and nothing has worked. It's out of my hands."

There was silence on the other end of the line. The guidance counselor solemnly said, "Thank you for your time, Mrs. Peabody," and hung up.

Amazingly enough Karl's next report card showed a marked improvement. Eventually he made the honor roll. His senior year, Susan attended a parent-teacher conference with Karl. The teachers marveled at the way he had turned himself around. She was so grateful for this answer to her desperate prayer. On the way home Karl said, "Mom, you remember that call from the guidance counselor last year?"

Susan nodded.

"That was me. I thought I'd play a joke but when I heard what you said, it really hit me how much I was hurting you. That's when I knew I had to make you proud."

Give yourself a time, pick a place and pray. Do it a little bit every day. Check in. God will find you wherever you are and you can find God. You don't have to say much. "Hi, God" will do. At that long-ago youth service at church when I was close to Karl's age, my voice barely changed, my shirt rumpled, my sideburns just wishful thinking, I walked down the aisle with the rest of the group. We passed out daisies on the way. Some of the girls danced in leotards at the altar. We played Simon and Garfunkel's "Bridge Over Troubled Water" because we knew how precious friendships were. Then I said my prayer.

A small shock wave passed over the congregation's bowed heads, like a breeze ruffling a mountain lake. But that generation gap we talked about in those days was mostly a figment of our imaginations. I remember one of the older members of the congregation coming up to me after the service, clutching my hand in a cloud of perfume. "I don't always say it the way you do, but when I pray it's just like a conversation with my best friend. I think that's what you meant, wasn't it?"

Oh, to be heard. Oh, to be understood.

## CHAPTER THREE

# Pray for Others

*"Be with those I love and the ones they love…"*

When you're not sure what to pray or how to pray, say a prayer for someone else.

John Howard works for Lowe's near his home in Elizabethtown, Kentucky. One November morning, earlier than usual, he got in his Ford pickup, grabbed a cup of coffee at the drive-through and took a shortcut through a new subdivision. In the pre-dawn darkness he spotted a glow up ahead. He thought maybe somebody put up Christmas decorations early, but no, it was a big piece of plywood, about four feet by three feet, painted white with a message bathed in floodlights: "Please pray for Baby Layne."

Questions bounced around in his mind: Who was this Baby Layne? What was wrong with Baby Layne? And who would go to the trouble of putting up a lighted sign asking for prayer?

John wasn't a particularly religious guy and not very confident in his prayers. Praying felt pretty mechanical and he wasn't even sure God heard him or would answer, but there was something about the honesty of this request on its plywood background that touched him. He would pray for Baby Layne, whoever Baby Layne was.

It became his morning routine. Get into the truck, grab some coffee at the drive through, cut through the subdivision, slow down at the sign and pray for Baby Layne. He finally told his wife, Susan, about it and what he'd been doing. Like many wives, she was a little more practiced in prayer and often prayed for others. "Isn't it nice to start your day by thinking about someone else?" she said.

"I just wonder how Baby Layne is doing," John said.

"Why don't you knock on their door and ask?" she said.

He didn't want to bother a family caring for a sick child, and anyway what would he say? That praying for a complete stranger had helped him? That keeping this regular appointment with God was a comfort and a blessing? Besides it was so early in the morning when he passed the house. Better to say nothing.

Then one spring afternoon, on his way home from Lowe's, he passed the house and sign and saw a man out in front. Fiftyish like him, in a white baseball cap, mowing the lawn. *Now's my chance,* John thought. He pulled into the driveway and got out of his truck. The man reached down to shut off his lawn mower.

John hesitated for a moment. I know exactly how he must have felt. Do you really want to tell some complete stranger that you've been praying for him or for his family? Doesn't it sound completely outlandish? And who are you to think your prayers mean anything?

How presumptuous of you, how intrusive, how foolish. But John had stepped out of the pickup truck.

"I just wanted to tell you," he said. "I... I saw your sign a few months back and I've been praying for Baby Layne ever since."

The man in the white baseball cap stood there; then his eyes pooled with tears. "I'm Kenny," he said. "Baby Layne is my grandson and hearing that really means a lot, sir. Thank you." Then he gave John a bear hug.

There is a sublime intimacy to praying for someone else that breaks down all barriers. Jesus exhorted us to do it, even saying that we should pray for our enemies: "Love your enemies, bless them that curse you, do good to them that hate you, and pray for them which despitefully use you, and persecute you." What a challenge that is. Praying for strangers seems a good deal easier.

I love the Apostle Paul's expressions of prayer. What he writes in his letter to the Philippians, a letter that's almost two thousand years old, sounds as fresh as an e-mail I got yesterday: "I thank my God every time I remember you, constantly praying with joy in every one of my prayers for all of you" (Philippians 1:3). What a way to say "I'm keeping you in my prayers." Nothing perfunctory about it. His passionate tone fills me with awe. "And this is my prayer, that your love may overflow more and more with knowledge and full insight to help you to determine what is best, so that in the day of Christ you may be pure and blameless, having produced the harvest of righteousness that comes through Jesus Christ for the glory and praise of God" (Philippians 1:9–10). What a model for prayer. Go out on a limb when you pray for others.

Take a risk. Be outrageous. Be passionate. Wish for the biggest thing you could possibly wish for. Take a leap. Love a lot not just a little. My friend Rick Thyne sometimes calls me from California in the middle of the day, in between clients in his psychotherapy practice. "Just thinking of you and Carol," he'll say. "You know how much I love you both. Hugs, prayers." I feel like one of those Philippians or Corinthians, anyone who received one of Paul's letters must have felt, zapped by outrageous love. In the unguarded language of faith Rick refers to me as one of his "beloveds," part of his spiritual community. Of course he struggles in his faith. He's faced devastating losses. Lord knows, he's stumbled more than a few times, but this is what he does. He prays for people whenever he can. His patients are blanketed in prayer whether they know it or not (most of them probably don't). It's his gift to them, an essential part of his work.

The truth of the matter is that when you pray for someone else, you're helping yourself. Love is disinterested but love has this side benefit of making you bigger, stronger, less selfish, more interesting—in a word, lovelier. Praying for others is a bellwether of mental health for me. If I'm sinking into self-absorption, if I'm worried too much about what's happening to me, I know what to do. Pray, for goodness' sake. Pray for myself, yes, because I can't avoid that (no use hiding my feelings). Then pray for somebody else. Pray for all those who need God so much more than me. Dad always put it in his graces, "Be with those we love and the ones they love..." and he'd name a few. He'd tell them too, "I'm holding a good thought for you."

You should see my desk, littered with yellow Post-It notes with names of people I'm praying for: "Jerry, chemo…Emma, loss…Emily, healthy baby…Roberta's girls…David, job interview…Monty, business…Rebecca, job…Renee, lawsuit…Pat, peace…Chuck, addiction…Mary Lou, ankle…" I'm not great at it but I just keep doing it. You just do. Thank God for e-mail. I can send a quick e-mail with a follow-up question—"How are you? You're in my prayers"—and keep track, updating the Post-It notes.

I know, I know. It can be embarrassing and cringe-making to tell someone that you're praying for them, especially people who don't believe in prayer and think it's utter nonsense or worse, delusional. "You're in my thoughts," I'll say, or borrowing Dad's language, "I'm holding a good thought for you." I've been known to put it in all caps— "HOW ARE YOU?"—because the prayer feels so urgent, a shout-out to God. The pain is immediate, the worry grave. I have to trust that all the people I pray for know it's out of love. Affection and fondness can cover a world of awkwardness. May my agnostic friends, whom I adore, forgive me if my prayers seem presumptuous or intrusive. "Be with those we love and the ones they love" is a crucial part of prayer.

I've even turned my prayer list into a memory exercise. Forgetfulness has been a problem of late, a sure sign of age. Coming up with people's names is the worst. I sputter and draw a blank. If Carol's anywhere close I turn to her for help: "You know who I'm talking about, honey. That guy we went to college with who played hockey and used to go out with what's her name and then got married to her roommate instead…" She usually *does* know who I'm talking about. She's my hard drive for names, but like a good wife she'll wait as I go through my game of Twenty Questions. She makes me search my own hard drive just to see if it's running.

"Memorize the names on your prayer list," I told myself. "It'll be good for your spiritual life and good for your aging brain."

I put the names in groups of five. Easier to remember that way. I'll look at one of my Post-It notes, then close my eyes and go down the list in my head. The mental search is part of the prayer. Who e-mailed me the other day? Who is struggling? Who is going through a rough patch? Who asked me to pray? I can almost feel myself opening a file in my brain, one of compassion and care, one that needs plenty of use or it would disappear.

On that spring day in Kentucky, John got the whole story about Baby Layne. Kenny's grandson had been born four months premature, weighing just over a pound, and had to have open-heart surgery. "The doctors didn't think he would make it," Kenny said, "but I wanted to do something to help so I made the sign." Look what happened. A guy found a prayer routine on his morning commute. A premature baby survived. And two strangers became friends.

Baby Layne is a healthy kid now, running around on his grandfather's lawn. John and his wife drop by to see him and his grandfather. And all because of how John responded to a simple request on a plywood sign.

◆ ◆ ◆

Prayer expands your world. You learn to care about people you would never have known otherwise, and you find out what makes them tick.

You grow in your ability to love. I have a Facebook friend I pray for. She's suffered some setbacks over the years and reached out to me, so I added her to my list. Following her on Facebook can be alarming. She posts and links to stuff that seems outrageous to me—polemical screeds. Every time I'm ready to hit the delete button, there's an inner voice that urges me, *Maybe there's something important here that you need to understand. Grow. Listen. Learn.* We all live in our little bubbles and certainly the New York City bubble I inhabit can seem mighty small and parochial (funny, how a city of eight million can be small). Prayer stretches me and takes me outside of my limited universe.

River Jordan is a novelist in Tennessee. Her two sons were in the military and a couple of years ago at Christmastime she learned that both boys were going to be deployed, one to Afghanistan, one to Iraq. She was devastated. What if this was their last Christmas as a family? What if this was the last time she saw them together? How was she going to get through this year that they were gone?

Then she had one of those crazy, out-of-the-blue, wake-up-in-the-middle-of-the-night inspirations. For her New Year's resolution she decided that she would pray for at least one stranger for every day that her boys were gone. Raising the stakes, she decided she should also, whenever possible, tell the strangers that she was praying for them.

This seemed like an impossible challenge, harder than promising to lose fifty pounds in the new year. River is an introvert, a self-described "say-my-prayers-in-private" kind of person. How was she going to handle going up to a stranger and saying, "I'm praying for you"? Why had she ever made such a difficult New Year's resolution? The first time she did it she was at the bus terminal in Nashville. She felt drawn to the woman at the ticket counter. Mustering up all her courage, she walked up to the woman and said, "Hi, my name is River...and I have this resolution to pray for a stranger every day, and today you're my stranger so I'll be thinking about you and saying special prayers for you."

The woman was stunned. "Oh, honey! My name is Annie. This is unbelievable! Do you know what I was saying to God just this morning?"

"No, ma'am..."

"I was saying my prayers when I asked God, 'Is there anybody in this whole wide world who is praying for me?'"

"Well, it looks like I am," River said.

Pretty unbelievable. All that year, every day, she'd look for a stranger to pray for. As she says, "I can't say I chose them exactly. Sometimes it seemed like they were chosen for me. I'd turn the corner and a person would come into view and it was like an inexplicable urging: *This is the one.*"

Sometimes River thought she'd chosen the wrong stranger, like the time she was in a restaurant and her eyes landed on a gorgeous young woman wearing killer shoes and an artfully tied scarf. Not exactly a "please pray for me" poster child, she seemed to have everything together. But River felt drawn to pray for her. Only when she talked to her did she discover that this "Miss Perfect" was a victim of the economy, out of work and worried whether she'd find a job.

Appearances can be deceiving. Everybody needs prayer, as River said, "even beautiful women wearing designer shoes."

Keeping her New Year's resolution forced River Jordan to get out and meet people. She couldn't get swallowed up in her worries. She was constantly discovering what other people's worries were, what kept them up at night. Her own prayers were answered when both her sons came home after a year of deployment. By then, though, praying for strangers had become an essential part of her life and well-being. She's still at it.

I'll admit that when I read River's story I told myself, "She could do that because she lives in the South, near the buckle of the Bible Belt. Everybody talks about prayer down there, but I live in New York. No one's going to buy that from me. No stranger will want to know I'm praying for them."

Then one summer day I was sitting on the steps in front of a sky-scraper and a young guy sat near me and started to talk. Unlike River, I am no introvert but the son of a man who always assumed that eleva-tor operators, concierges, desk clerks and hardware salesmen wanted to be asked about more than the weather. Mind you, New Yorkers also like to talk. This guy told me how tough his job was and how awful his boss was and how he wasn't sure he could take it anymore. The stress was terrible. He feared he wasn't measuring up. He might never succeed.

"Do you have a family?" I asked. "Anybody who cares about you?"

"Yes," he said. "My girlfriend cares."

"Maybe you can remember that when things are stressful," I suggested.

"I'll try."

"It also helps to come outside and take a break like you're doing now, doesn't it? It's really a beautiful day."

"Yeah, it is."

At this point I took a big breath and asked, "What's your name?"

"John," he said.

"Okay, John, I'll pray for you." I stood up and shook his hand, and his name went on a Post-It note.

As I mentioned, praying for others is how we start our week at the Guideposts offices.

I remember the first time I did it, 9:45 on a Monday morning, sitting at the conference room table. I reached for a stack of the letters our readers had sent in. I rolled up my sleeves and began reading. What a catalog of suffering and misery. In those days the letters were mostly handwritten and you could see a world of pain in small, jittery handwriting or desperation in harried script on yellow lined paper. Cancer, death, divorce, job loss, alcoholism, addiction, financial troubles, family issues, marriage struggles, grief, imprisonment, infertility, infidelity. I quickly learned to search for the letter that expressed gratitude for a blessing or asked for something comparatively minor, like the teenager who wanted us to pray that she make it to cheerleading camp.

But I still have the same feeling I had that first day. Like River Jordan, I'm incredibly grateful for my blessings.

Today most of the requests come through the Internet, tens of thousands of them every month. We have hundreds of volunteers around the world praying. Every request gets prayed for at least once. Nobody has to pay. (Yes, there are sites that will charge you for prayer!) If you want to read some touching prayer requests—and people's answers to prayer—visit OurPrayer.org. Try it when you're having a bad day. One scroll down through the heartache of others will convince you how blessed you are and remind you that you are not alone in your struggles.

"Hi, I am so devastated about giving my dog away," came one recent request. "I believed with all my heart that I was doing the right thing. I believe he went to a home that could give him more than I could. But I loved my dog and miss him so much. It has been two months now and I cry almost every day. I want to get over this and I have prayed that God will heal my broken heart. Next to the Lord, he was my best friend. Please pray for me."

Ouch.

"I am going through a hard time right now. My husband is having an affair with a woman at his job. He comes home late every night. My daughter is a senior in high school and told him about her awards ceremony, but he didn't show up. What have I done wrong? Please keep us in your prayers."

Ugh.

"Please pray for my friend. He hasn't been able to find work for two years now. No public program seems able to reach him or help him. He is behind on his electric bill and his rent. He is pitiful and angry.

I can't help him anymore. Please, any prayers and kind thoughts for him would be MUCH appreciated. I did not tell him I am doing this but I think that is okay."

I prayed for all of them. Every week I pray for requests like these. A priest at our church, Elizabeth Maxwell, used a helpful phrase when she described prayer as a process to help us metabolize sorrow. Without prayer, sorrows can make us bitter. With prayer, we can transform sorrow and anger into empathy, understanding, compassion. Every Monday I take on that task.

And yet, I can still feel I'm not up to it or that really somebody else should be doing it, somebody more qualified. Our volunteers, mind you, get training.

One busy morning at work the phone rang. An unfamiliar number was on the caller ID but I answered it. (Just so you know how easily distracted I am, I always answer my phone. I always think, "Maybe it's one of my kids calling from some unknown number.") "Hello," I said in a brisk businesslike tone.

"I'm Bernadette," a faint voice said.

"This is Rick Hamlin. Can I help you?" I asked, searching my memory to see if I knew a Bernadette. Someone whose story I had worked on? Someone who had sent me a manuscript?

"I need someone to pray with me," she said. "My friend Mary is very, very sick from cancer and is in hospice care. I don't know what to do. I'll miss her so much..." She sounded like she was crying.

In addition to OurPrayer online, we have volunteers and employees who will pray for people on the phone. Clearly this woman needed to be transferred to someone who could help her, someone who'd been trained to. What number should I give her? I looked at my bulletin board. Where had I written that down?

"Tell me more about your friend," I said, stalling.

She went on and everything she said—how quickly the cancer had spread, how hard it was to know whether to pray for a miracle or a quick passing, how alone she felt—told me that it would be the biggest cop-out to bounce this grieving woman around, to put her on hold or ask her to dial another line. Maybe she'd gotten my number for a reason.

"Can I pray with you right now?" I finally asked.

"Yes," she said.

I did my best, lowering my voice, saying what came into my head. Did I help? I don't know. I hope so. I do know it was the right thing to do.

◆ ◆ ◆

When you get to be known, however modestly, as a praying person, people will ask you quite openly if you will pray for them. I worry all the time that I will forget to pray for someone I've promised to pray for. Hence the Post-It notes. It doesn't work just to say, "I'll remember." I might, I might not. Any reminders are good. Over a decade ago, when we got new computers at the office, we were told that we needed to change our passwords every month. I did okay for a while, using some variation of my name, my kids' names, my wife's names, everybody's birthdays, my mom and dad's birthdays. Eventually I ran out of good mnemonic methods. Then I looked at my prayer list.

"Use someone on the prayer list for your password," I decided. I typed in a name. The next morning, of course, I couldn't remember why I couldn't log on. Then I thought, "Who are you praying for?" Bingo. Thirty days is a good time period to pray for someone. They're not going to necessarily be out of trouble or on easy street in thirty days, but their situation will definitely have changed. It's always satisfying to retire a name. Prayer answered.

For many years my dad was a volunteer for the Tournament of Roses, the organization that puts on the Rose Bowl and Rose Parade in Pasadena. He rose up through the ranks, directing traffic, managing crowds, checking on the safety of the floats, going to endless meetings. In the early eighties he became the vice president. What was his job that year? They told him he was in charge of the weather.

Now, as anyone who has seen the Rose Parade and Rose Bowl on TV knows: it's always on the first of the year. (Except when January 1 happens to be a Sunday, then it becomes a moveable feast, the wise souls of the Tournament believing the Sabbath should be observed.) And it's always beautiful weather. At that point it hadn't rained on a parade in nearly thirty years, not since the year I was born.

"Thornt," they told my dad, "you've got a good relationship with the Almighty. You make sure it doesn't rain."

What do you know? The skies on New Year's Eve that year were gray and cloudy. Shortly after midnight the rains came down, one of those torrential storms that surprise you in balmy Southern California. The people camped out on the parade route huddled under umbrellas and tarps. The waiting floats were covered with plastic to protect the flowers, the bands put on their foul-weather gear, and the queen and her court were issued umbrellas.

But just on the dot of eight, when the parade started heading down Orange Grove Boulevard, the sun came out. Another beautiful day.

"Good job, Thornt," Dad's pals told him. "You've got friends in high places." I can see Dad's blue eyes crinkle and hear him murmur modestly, "I was just holding a good thought." Good prayers come with a dose of humility and awe.

Why should our prayers convince the Almighty to do something he'd want to do anyway? Why should a thousand prayers change his mind? I suspect it's not about God but about us. God wants us to pray for others because it helps us focus on what's most important and brings out the good in others in us. It spreads hope. It reverses the momentum of despair and pain. God doesn't need to hear from us to be convinced. But we need to reach out and speak up, to convince ourselves. We become co-laborers with God. We welcome the sun or meet the rain. For the person prayed for, it's an extraordinary gift. When you've been on the other end you feel it.

Lee Woodruff and her husband, Bob, went through a terrible ordeal but as far as they're concerned they wouldn't have gotten through it without the prayers of others. Lots of others.

I met Lee and Bob in their sun-drenched Westchester, New York, kitchen a year after he'd been wounded in Iraq. Bob is a reporter for ABC News, and he'd gone to Iraq in his role as co-anchor of the evening news. He and his cameraman were filming a segment from a tank hatch, on the lookout for insurgents, when the tank hit a roadside

IED. As they say, you never hear the bomb that hits you, and Bob didn't. But as his body fell back into the tank, he remembered being enveloped by a pure white light and floating above it. Then he was on the floor of the tank, spitting up blood. That was the last thing he knew.

Lee was at Disney World with their four children that January morning when she got the call. The president of ABC News gave her the news, choosing his words very carefully. "Bob has been wounded in Iraq. He's alive but he may have taken shrapnel to the brain." He was being flown to a military hospital in Germany.

This was Bob's fifth trip to Iraq. Going to dangerous places was part of his job. Lee had learned to put the worst of her fears out of her mind, to avoid them as much as possible. She was busy enough taking care of the children. But now it looked like the worst of her fears had come true. A head wound, shrapnel to the brain. Would Bob survive? She wanted to shout out to God, "Why us?"

She flew back with the children to New York. A network of friends and family stepped in to help while Lee went to Germany. Nothing could have prepared her for that first sight of her husband in the ICU. His head was swollen to the size of a rugby ball, deformed at the top where a piece of his skull was missing. There were cuts and stitches on his cheeks, forehead and neck. His lips were swollen. His left eye looked like a dead fish, she said. He was unconscious. She leaned down to kiss him and spoke, hoping he somehow heard: "I love you, sweetie. You've had an accident, but you're going to be all right."

The doctors were guarded. Bob was young and in good shape. He could recover. But for the first time Lee heard a phrase that would be repeated again and again over the next thirty-five days: "It takes a long time for the brain to heal. Remember this is a marathon, not a sprint."

She couldn't fly with Bob to the hospital in Bethesda, Maryland. Traveling on her own, she handed her passport to the customs agent through the Plexiglas window. The woman looked at it and her face softened. She handed the passport back and squeezed Lee's hands. "The nation's thoughts and prayers are with you, Mrs. Woodruff," she said. It was Lee's first indication of the prayer support she'd get.

In Bethesda Lee started a routine that would last weeks. She'd go to the ICU in the morning and talk to Bob in that overly cheery voice a mother uses with her baby. She would let him know about the kids and tell him stories of how they met. She would play music for him. His eyes were blank, his face expressionless. *Somewhere there's a brain in there healing,* she tried to remind herself.

Then she'd go to the YMCA for a swim, talking to God as she did her laps. Would she be all right? What about the kids? What would Bob be like when he woke up? The doctors and nurses had warned her, "Prepare yourself, Mrs. Woodruff. Bob will have to learn things all over again. Think of him as a baby learning to speak, then read and write..."

The prayers kept coming, e-mails, notes, cards, a cross that he could hold in his hand, homemade angels made out of paper clips. "We're praying for you," people said, praying in churches, synagogues, mosques, community centers, living rooms and YMCAs. Lee read the notes to Bob and hung some of the cards up on the hospital room wall. When her own faith felt weak she turned to the faith of others.

One day when the children were visiting, Bob's older daughter kissed him and Lee saw a tear roll down his cheek. Wasn't that a sign of hope? Another time as she sat next to him, talking to him, telling him, "I love you, I'm with you," he grew agitated. He seemed to be trying to talk through the tracheotomy tube. He pulled her hand towards him and she was sure he mouthed the words, "I love you, sweetie." The nurse had to give him a shot to calm him down. Lee clung to that image of him trying to speak as much as she clung to the prayers on the walls around them.

The fourth week the trache tube came out and Bob was moved to another ward. Lee felt her own energy flagging. She missed being with her children back in New York. Their visits to Bethesda were too short and too few. Her fears of the future haunted her. The conversations with God on her morning swim grew desperate. Doctors warned her that Bob's personality might have changed because of the brain injury. What if he were violent when he woke up? What if he didn't know who she was? He'd grown so thin and fragile. How much longer could she go on?

She went for an early swim one morning, then headed to Bob's hospital room. She pushed open the door and froze. He was sitting up in bed, a big smile on his face. He saw her and lifted his hands in the air. "Hey, sweetie," he said, "where have you been?" Overjoyed, incredulous, she wanted to say the same thing back to him: *Where have YOU been?*

There were many months of therapy ahead. Bob came back to New York and spent his days as an inpatient at Columbia University Medical Center. He would struggle to find a word and Lee got good at playing charades, but when he came up with something like "unsettling" all on his own, she knew he was well on his way. Bob was back.

You don't go through something like that without being changed. For Lee she gained a new understanding of the power of prayer. When she was weak, when she was struggling, when she feared she was at the end of her rope, others were thoughtful enough to pray for her. They covered for her. They gave her strength.

◆ ◆ ◆

When I talked to Lee Woodruff about her story I must have said something about Columbia University Medical Center. It's a sprawling complex in upper Manhattan and we live only fifteen blocks away. After a few years of having doctors all over the city, we figured it would be good to find a primary care physician who was affiliated with Columbia, who could refer us to any of the specialists there. Worst-case scenario, if anything went wrong in the family, we would have a hospital with doctors we knew nearby.

A couple of months after Lee's story came out in *Guideposts*, one of those doctors, a lung specialist, was worried about a chest X-ray I'd had and sent me for a CT scan. On a cool sunny November Saturday I walked down to the hospital for the exam and walked home. That afternoon I planted my tulip bulbs in the little garden in front of our apartment. I wasn't thinking about my health. I was more concerned about making sure the bulbs were deep enough so the squirrels wouldn't get to them. I was a little alarmed when the specialist called

Carol at home—the only number she had—and told her I should call back immediately. "Your lungs look fine," the specialist said, "but you've got an aneurysm in your aorta that looks really big. You'd better do something about it."

A tremor of fear passed through me. An aneurysm? In my aorta? Didn't people die when an aneurysm burst? I'd always had a heart murmur, an indication of a defective valve. I went to a cardiologist every two years just to get it looked at. He'd told me there was a weakness to the walls of my aorta and this could cause major trouble someday, but I didn't think much of it. After all, I was in good shape. I ate well, got plenty of exercise, had strikingly low cholesterol levels. An aneurysm? He never mentioned that was a possibility.

The next thing I knew I was in my cardiologist's office and he was tapping his yellow pencil on his desk and using it to point out the aorta in a large model of the heart. "You'll need to have open-heart surgery," he said. "And soon."

Fear swept over me like a cold wind. Open-heart surgery would be a huge ordeal. I'd be under anesthesia for hours, lying on a table in the operating room. The idea of it gave me the creeps. A machine would take over for my heart and lungs. I wouldn't even be breathing on my own.

"Isn't there some less invasive way of doing this?" I asked.

"No," he said simply.

I headed back to work. On the subway I took out my green pocket Bible. I turned to the Psalms and tried to pray. But nothing would come. The rhythm of the cars careening along the track, the usual background for my spiritual ritual, jarred me and cranked up my fears. All I could think of was being in that operating room, unconscious, cut off from the world, cut off from God.

I called my old college roommate Jim. He and I have prayed each other through tons of situations over the years. We're godparents to each other's kids. "It looks like I'm going to have to have open-heart surgery." I filled him in.

"We'll keep you in our prayers," he said.

I talked to Carol that night. Open-heart surgery. Soon. Maybe in an attempt to deal with her own fears, she told a few friends and relatives the news and it spread like wildfire. Family and friends e-mailed her and then more friends e-mailed back, asking to be put on her list for updates. Her collection of e-mail addresses started to look like a Christmas card list gone haywire. We heard from people we hadn't seen in years, friends from college and high school, parents from our boys' kindergarten days.

Two days before the operation, we met with my surgeon in his office. Still wearing his scrubs, fresh from surgery, he gave us a PowerPoint presentation on how he'd repair my aorta and replace the defective valve. It was a polished talk, meant to allay my fears. "I do this operation two hundred times a year," he said, "and I've never lost a patient." *Of course,* that made me think, *I could be the first.* I knew my rising panic wasn't rational. I trusted the surgeon, the hospital. But to tell yourself a fear is irrational doesn't make it go away. I couldn't get out of my head the image of me with a machine pumping my blood and breathing for me while I lay there dead to the world.

I checked into the hospital and got prepped for surgery, my chest shaved and marked as though my heart were a bull's-eye. Carol brought me a big salad for dinner and the nurses were in and out of my room, checking my blood pressure, monitoring my heart. But then they all left.

I lay there in the cardiac ward feeling very much alone, unable to sleep, unable to pray. I turned to a prayer I've relied on for years: "Jesus Christ, have mercy on me. Rescue me and save me. Let thy will be done in my life." But that night saying those familiar words, I felt no sense of spiritual connection. All I felt was fear.

Carol came by in the morning with a friend who promised to distract both of us. We talked about everything but surgery. All too soon visiting hours were over. Carol kissed me and was gone. The nurse came for my things. I took one last look at my Bible and handed it over. Any minute now I'd have to go to the operating room and be put under. I almost didn't answer the phone when it rang. "Hello," I said.

"Rick," came a warm, familiar voice.

"Tibby!" My friend the writer Elizabeth Sherrill and her husband, John, on the other line.

"You are the last person I would ever expect to be in the hospital for heart surgery," she said.

"That's what I thought," I said.

"How are you?" she asked.

"Pretty anxious," I admitted. "I didn't sleep at all last night. I keep thinking about the anesthesia and being on the heart-lung machine. It's like being dead. I can't even pray."

"We'll pray for you."

John and Tibby did pray for me, right there on the phone. I didn't say anything. I let go and let their words do the work for me. What I couldn't do for myself, others would do for me. I would depend on all the people who had promised to pray for me. They would keep me connected to God. Just as a machine would do the work of my heart and lungs, I could trust my friends and family to do the work of my soul.

That moment, waiting for the techs and their gurney to take me to the OR, closing my eyes and clutching a phone, was a revelation. That's why I take very seriously the request, "Keep me in your prayers." Praying has a huge effect on the object of those prayers, all the better if they know it. When your connection to God is fraying, there are others who will keep you in touch. When you can't pray for yourself, let someone else pray for you.

"Amen," Tibby and John said.

"Amen," I echoed.

The surgery was a success. These days I go to the gym, I run a lot and I eat carefully. And I try not to miss an opportunity to pray for anybody who needs it.

## CHAPTER FOUR

# Praying the Lord's Prayer

*"Our Father, who art in heaven, hallowed be thy name..."*

I'm not the first person, and I trust I won't be the last, to point out that the Lord's Prayer is in the first-person plural. It's not "Give me this day my daily bread" or "Deliver me from evil" or "Forgive me my sins" (or my debts or my trespasses) "as I forgive those who sin against me." It's "give us," "deliver us" and "forgive us." We're in this together. What we ask for ourselves, we ask for others. When we say "Our Father, who art in heaven..." we're not alone. Even if you pray it by yourself on a deserted island, you're including yourself in the community of faith with every word. "Wherever two or three are gathered together in my name," Jesus famously said, "there I am in the midst of them" (Matthew 18:20, KJV). The very words of the Lord's Prayer echo that thought.

Praying with others is different than praying by yourself. I don't focus half as well when I'm in a pew praying with people around me. It feels like I'm closer to God when I'm all by myself, bombarding him with my worries, closing my eyes with the words of a psalm on my lips. We have Jesus' example of going off by himself. After feeding the five thousand, "He went up on the mountain to pray" (Matthew 6:46). No wonder. Multiplying the loaves and fishes must have been a lot of work, not to mention talking to all those people afterwards. (The coffee hour to end all coffee hours.) But then he also prayed with his disciples, showing them how to pray together.

The Lord's Prayer appears twice in the Bible. In each case the context and set up is a little different. As Luke describes it, Jesus was praying, apparently by himself, and when he had finished one of the disciples asked him, "Lord, teach us how to pray the way John taught his disciples" (Luke 11:1, CEB).

Jesus responded, "When you pray, say" and then he gave the disciples the familiar words "Our Father…"

In the book of Matthew the prayer appears towards the end of that good advice usually called the Sermon on the Mount. Jesus is urging the disciples not to pray ostentatiously with long empty phrases and lots of words.

"Do not be like them," he says, "for your Father knows what you need before you ask him. Pray then in this way…" And he gives his listeners the Lord's Prayer. In this case it seems more like a guide. *Pray in this way* vs. *When you pray, say*. It's as though Jesus is urging his disciples, here's what you should do when you pray: Be direct. Make it simple. Don't be long-winded. Cover all the bases. Forgive. Relinquish. Pray for others as you pray for yourself.

A guide for prayer or the specific words of a prayer, it works both ways. What Jesus must have realized is that we humans need something to hold on to, words we can use in any situation, a lifeline of phrases, even though he's assured us that God hears us before we say anything. I can almost see him rolling his eyes at the disciples, thinking, "O ye of little faith, if you really need something, here it is."

Guess what? We do need it.

Talking to people over the years, hearing their stories, I'm often surprised how the Lord's Prayer doesn't necessarily feel like the right prayer, but it's the only one they can think of. And it's effective. I remember one woman, a hard-driving New York real estate developer who was constantly in tough negotiations. She drummed her manicured fingernails impatiently on her desk as we talked and scowled at a ringing phone. I wouldn't have wanted to be on her bad side. Once, in the middle of a deal when she was sure she was being cheated, she was so angry she knew she needed to calm down or she simply couldn't function. "Pray, pray," she told herself. But what could she pray? "The Lord's Prayer," she thought, even though it had no apparent connection to getting the loan or dealing with her colleague's machinations.

"I stood outside that conference room and pretended to rummage through my briefcase while I said the Lord's Prayer to myself. You know what?" she said to me. "I couldn't come up with the words. I was too angry. It took me a whole minute to remember, 'Our Father, who art in heaven…' In that time I was able to collect myself and go back to the meeting."

"What happened with the colleague?" I asked.

"Later he apologized. It was a misunderstanding. I don't work with him anymore, which is just as well, but we're friends."

"What about the loan?"

"I got it," she said with a crisp smile.

She felt all alone, trapped by her feelings, then reached for the Lord's Prayer. It was that very act, searching for the words when she couldn't find them, that gave her a necessary measure of peace.

Back in the 1980s, Elaine St. Johns, a writer I worked with when I first came to the magazine, got a call at midnight from a friend of a friend. "Walt has had a massive heart attack," the woman said. "Mona wanted me to let you know. They're in an ambulance right now. Mona said, 'Pray for us.'"

The shock of the news, the fear, made Elaine's well of prayer run dry. All she could think of was her friend Mona sitting by her stricken husband Walt. Elaine could picture the ambulance rushing to the hospital. She could envision the doctors and nurses scurrying back and forth in the ER. The prospect of loss devastated her and made prayer impossible.

"Help me pray," she asked God. Quick as lightning the thought came to her: *Pray the Lord's Prayer.* Just as quickly her mind rejected the idea. She'd said the Lord's Prayer many times. She'd prayed it often with Mona. But it didn't speak to the current situation. There was nothing in it about illness or racing ambulances and raging fears. *PRAY the Lord's Prayer*, the inner voice said again. This time she obeyed, and prayed the familiar words more carefully and thoughtfully than ever before. She paused over each phrase.

This was before the era of cell phones and e-mail. Elaine didn't find out what happened for several days. At first the prognosis looked dire. Walt not only had suffered a heart attack but also had three clots in his lungs, pneumonia and a temperature of 107 degrees.

But Walt recovered. Better yet, he became a different person. He had been "a borderline agnostic," but after that night there was a complete change in his attitude toward God. Elaine didn't think it was coincidental.

She continued to pray the Lord's Prayer slowly and intentionally as she had that night. The results were satisfying, and as she said, often unexpected. An ugly tumor, scheduled for surgery, simply disappeared from her finger. A financial crisis and a family squabble of some duration both evaporated without her taking any action or giving it further thought.

"There is no way to pray this prayer for one person or one family alone," she wrote. "The minute I consciously addressed 'Our Father,' even though my immediate concern was Walt and Mona, I was also including my family, friends, strangers, enemies. I was praying for them as well. As I contemplated this I realized the universal intent of Christ when he gave the prayer to us. When we pray 'Thy kingdom come, thy will be done on earth as it is in heaven,' we make supplication not only for our own known and unknown needs but also for the needs of his children everywhere. This, to me, was the source of those unexpected results in my own experience—the healing of my finger, my finances, my family relationships. The implications on a worldwide scale were overwhelming."

My mother first taught us the Lord's Prayer when we were kids gathered around the teak table in the lanai, the dog looking quizzically at us through the sliding glass doors, waiting for his dinner. We'd finished ours. A lifelong learner and a budding Sunday school teacher, Mom wanted us to know this one prayer, her blessing to us. We repeated the words after her, Dad at her side. It didn't take long to get it down. Perhaps we already knew it from church. What surprised me was her directive.

"You should pray this prayer whenever you're in trouble," she said. We nodded.

Never an alarmist, rarely given to think the worst, she still added, looking straight at Howard, "If you're in one of your forts and it falls down or if you're in a tunnel and it collapses, you can say this prayer." Howard was always building a stratospheric fort at the top of a swaying eucalyptus or digging a secret tunnel under the fence in the backyard, no doubt inspired by some movie we saw of POWs escaping from a Nazi prison camp. Perhaps her trust in the prayer's power could explain her usual equanimity. Still, I remember thinking, "Why all these big words? Wouldn't 'Help me, God' do just as well?"

Now I believe there's something to the way Elaine St. Johns put it. When you say the Lord's Prayer you're praying for your own needs, known and unknown, and praying for everyone else's too. You're making powerful links to your family and your community. Your helplessness is part of the world's helplessness, and your faith is shared with theirs. This feels like the foolishness of God that Paul writes about: "For God's foolishness is wiser than human wisdom and

God's weakness is stronger than human strength" (1 Corinthians 1:25). Jesus taught the prayer to us and we teach it to one another, passing it along from generation to generation. As any teacher knows, when you teach something, you learn it and your students become your teachers. If you've taught it to your children, they'll be sure to remind you of it.

On a May Sunday morning in 2010 there were terrible floods in Nashville. Services were canceled at the church Colleen Coury and her family usually attend. No one would be praying the Lord's Prayer there that morning. Colleen caught up on some work, but then realized they needed to do some shopping. The fridge was empty. She and her husband, Joe, and their twelve-year-old son, Clay, piled into their Chevy TrailBlazer for a quick grocery run.

The TrailBlazer's big all-weather tires gripped the road in the rain. It made it through a low spot near a creek, spraying water in all directions. Clay splashed through the puddles in the supermarket parking lot. They grabbed a few staples—a pound of turkey, a loaf of bread, a gallon of milk and a couple of pizzas—and were back in the Trail-Blazer in no time. Ten minutes and they'd be back home.

But when they came back to that low spot on the road, the puddle had swollen into what looked like a turbulent lake. Joe started to back up but there was a pickup right behind him. Figuring the water was about a foot deep, he eased the SUV forward. Halfway across, a wave rocked the truck and swamped the engine. Joe turned the key in the ignition. Dead. Colleen looked out her window. The water was halfway up the door.

Joe clicked his seatbelt loose, powered down the window—the electrical system still worked—and climbed into the churning water. It was waist deep. "Get out," he yelled to his son. "Hurry!" He helped Clay onto the hood. Colleen squeezed through the window and climbed onto the roof. Joe clung to the TrailBlazer's door. There was no room for him on the top of the truck.

Rescuers weren't far off. A fire truck pulled up and two men tethered to shore waded into the water and tossed them life vests. The current sucked the vests downstream. "I'm in trouble," Joe hollered. "I can't hold on much longer."

Colleen was starting to panic, fear surging through her. If her strong husband couldn't hang on much longer, how could she? Her hands were cold and trembling. Any moment she'd slide off the rain-slicked roof. She looked down at her son Clay, still on the hood. His eyes were closed, his head bowed. Then she heard him above the noise of the storm: "Our Father, who art in heaven, hallowed be thy name."

How many times had they said those words together? They were part of his bedtime ritual. She had taught Clay that prayer and now he was reminding her of just when to use it.

"Get on the roof!" Joe yelled to his son from the churning water. "Stay up there." Clay crawled up the windshield. "When the truck moves," Joe continued, "ride it to the trees, then jump off." With that he let go of the door.

The TrailBlazer began rocking. The current lifted it from the road and pushed it downstream like a bobbing cork. Colleen held her son tight. "Do something! Now!" she screamed to the rescue workers.

"Don't panic," they called back. How was that possible when her husband was clinging to a clump of ivy, his head barely above the water? The TrailBlazer was moving faster. It started tilting, capsizing. "Jump!" Joe yelled. "Get clear of it. Grab the first tree you can." The SUV sank from view.

Clay grabbed hold of some vines, and Colleen wrapped her arms around a small tree. Joe was yanked back into the current, grabbing a big elm leaning out into the water downstream. The water was cold. Colleen's heart was pounding. Then she heard Clay's voice again: "Our Father, who art in heaven..."

He was right. This was exactly what they should do. She prayed along with her twelve-year-old son. "Hallowed be thy name, thy kingdom come..." The words gave her some sort of hope.

"We're going to get through this," she yelled to Clay. "Keep praying."

"I'm getting tired," he said.

She saw a truck arriving with a small boat. "They're coming to get us. Just hold on a little longer!"

She was swept into the water, plunging helplessly into the current. Then she felt a hand grab her. Joe. She grabbed the trunk of the elm. Clay was sucked into the water too, but Joe was able to grab him. All three of them clung to the large elm.

Finally the men with the boat were able to get close enough to toss them life vests and a rope. They held onto the rope as they were pulled through the rapids to safety. The elm, the rope, the rescuers in the boat had saved them. But Colleen was quicker to say that prayer had been their lifeline. A prayer she had taught her son to say years earlier. A prayer they could say together.

◆ ◆ ◆

The Lord's Prayer pops up in the most unexpected places. Before writing this chapter I thumbed through stacks of back issues in my office—I've got loose copies of the magazine going back to 1977. I was amazed at how often the Lord's Prayer was a crucial part of the story. From home Bible studies to football huddles to AA meetings in church basements to people thrown together in natural disasters, the Lord's Prayer creates instant spiritual community. It provides healing words for what cannot always be said.

Roberta Rogers was not close to her father, "a complex and distant man," as she described him. She was vacationing on Topsail Island in North Carolina when she received news that at age eighty-four he had been diagnosed with inoperable cancer. Walking on the beach, where a rough tide had washed up hundreds of small stones and pieces of broken shell, she was reminded of the broken relationship she had with her dad. Losing him would mean also losing the hope that she would ever gain his unconditional love. The stiff sea breeze whipped through her hair. She looked down at the jagged-edged shells. A wave swept across the beach. Studying the sand, she bent down and picked up a few perfect shells.

Holding them in her hand she was able to recall a few untarnished memories. She remembered accompanying her dad on business trips when she was young and feeling important to be with him "calling on the trade." And there was the trip she and her brother took with him on the Mohawk Trail. Up early one morning they went for a walk on a misty country road and her dad showed them the flowers and told them their names. Once when she was eight she fell into a deep depression. It was the only time she remembered her dad opening up to her. He told her about his own fears and how he tried to believe God could help. His halting faith, so uncharacteristic of him to speak about, gave her hope.

Now, determined to keep hold of the good memories and let the other painful ones go, like the broken shells, she flew up to New England to be with her father. It wasn't a perfect visit. There was so much more she wanted to say but she couldn't find the words. She flew home. After that his condition deteriorated rapidly. He sank into a coma so deep he needed no painkillers, yet he held on tenaciously. One of the hospice nurses said she had never seen anyone survive so long in such a condition. It was as though he was waiting to see someone.

Roberta made one last trip. She sat next to her dad's bed and held his hand, listening to his hard, irregular breathing. She told him of those happy memories she had had, that walk along the country lane, the words he had used to comfort a frightened eight-year-old girl. A healing force flowed between them. Her brother joined them, sitting on the other side of the bed. They had never been a praying family, certainly never praying out loud, but the thought came to her: *We should pray the Lord's Prayer.* She fought the idea, but then her brother made the same suggestion. He whispered to their dad, "You want to say the Lord's Prayer." It was more a statement than a question.

For the first time they prayed together, "two of us loud and one silently," as Roberta said. "Our Father, who art in heaven...forgive us our trespasses as we forgive those who trespass against us..." all the way to the end of the prayer. Then she leaned over, kissed her Dad's brow and said, "I love you," the reconciliation she had longed for happening in an instance, all her remorse gone. The next day he died. The hospice nurse said he was at peace. So was Roberta.

Actor Ricardo Montalbán (of *Fantasy Island* fame) was appearing in the musical *Jamaica* on Broadway in the late fifties. The run of the show kept getting extended. At first his family was able to be with him, but they moved back to California and he felt marooned. Often he went to St. Malachy's Chapel with his dresser Charlie after the Saturday show. One Saturday he was fed up and lonely. When he knelt in the well-worn pews, all he could mutter was, "Lord, I want to go home. I miss my family." Then he heard Charlie pray, "Our Father..."

In those two small words was the reminder he needed. He was not alone. There were others he needed to look after. "Jesus, in teaching us how to pray, had made it clear that we were to speak not only for ourselves but for all members of his family—not just for me, Ricardo, but for all those around me," he wrote. The ache of homesickness melted away into caring for those he was with, like Charlie, like his cast members, like those worshiping in the chapel.

If you look into the different scientific studies testing the effectiveness of prayer, the results of some seem very helpful, proving that prayer offers benefits for a longer, healthier life. But the ones that strike me as foolish or in fact wrong are the ones that seek to set up controls—say, one group of hospital patients that will be prayed for and one group that will not, with researchers looking to see the differences between the two groups.

First of all, how do they know that the "un-prayed-for" really went without prayers? They might have had secret advocates that they didn't know about, never mind the researchers. Maybe we all do. Second, if I were a prayer volunteer in the study, I would have to point out that prayer is not something that limits itself to one small universe. Prayer is generous, indiscriminate, compassionate. It knows no bounds. How could you honestly say you are only going to pray for one group and not another? What kind of prayer would that be? Again, it's "Our Father," not "My Father."

Bill Butler and his wife, Simone, were lost at sea, a thousand miles from the nearest coastline. Their thirty-nine-foot sailboat had sunk and they were in an inflatable six-foot raft in the Pacific. As Bill put it, "Finding our little raft in this vast ocean would be like locating a Volkswagen Beetle somewhere between Florida and Oregon." Among the few crackers and canned goods on board Simone found some prayer cards. Time and again she would grasp Bill's hands and pray her way through the Lord's Prayer: "Our Father, who art in heaven…"

They caught fish with the one pole and hook they had. They drank water using a desalination pump. They fended off sharks and sea turtles. The sharks kept their distance during the day but at night they smacked the fragile raft with their tails and bumped it with their snouts as though it were a bath toy. The floor was so thin Bill and Simone could feel the sharks' snouts. One small tear in the raft would send it to the bottom of the ocean. *Whack!* A shark gave the raft a jolting blow with its tail. *Bang!* Another hit it from underneath, sending it spinning.

A huge freighter appeared out of nowhere and came so terrifyingly close that it almost rammed them. Despite Simone and Bill's screams, despite the flare they set off, the freighter rumbled on. The wind and water dragged them ever further from any shipping lanes. The sun beat down on them mercilessly. At night the sharks kept at it. Each day Bill managed to catch enough fish to keep them alive. Each day Simone grasped Bill's hands and said the Lord's Prayer. Initially Bill didn't join her—he wasn't a praying man or much of a believer, really—but as the weeks went on, he spoke out loud with her: "Thy kingdom come, thy will be done." It would take a miracle for them to survive.

After sixty-six days the currents brought them close to the shores of Costa Rica, where they were picked up by a patrol boat. Bill was a seasoned sailor with forty-eight years behind him. He knew how unlikely their survival was. "The odds against us making it were astronomical," he wrote. "Impossible even." They had lost weight, suffered terrible sunburn, their very clothes fraying on their emaciated bodies, but they lived. And from their prayers Bill found something he hadn't had when they first set off—a faith that gave him hope day after day. That prayer Simone said over and over became a part of him.

Julie Garmon is a forty-something mom with a son at home and two grown daughters. A prolific freelance writer, she works tirelessly at her craft and her faith. Recently she wrote about going to her yoga class after receiving discouraging news from her doctor. She'd been diagnosed with two autoimmune disorders—celiac disease and Sjögren's Syndrome—and she was scared. What would be next? How would her life change? Everything she read on the Internet only ratcheted up her worries. She almost skipped the class. Usually the different poses and the deep breathing served to clear her mind. Not that day. At the end of the class, she lay on her mat, still tense, when her teacher did something unexpected.

"Our Father, who art in heaven..." she began to say. Others joined in, saying the familiar words. Julie did too. Her mind calmed, her worries diminished. It was the only time her yoga teacher had ever prayed like that in class.

"Give us this day our daily bread" is a reminder not to worry about what will happen in the future. Sufficient unto the day. All we need to ask for is what we need today. I can get really worked up about stuff that's far off: Will I have enough for retirement? Will I be able to take care of my wife? Will I ever pay off my mortgage? Will I have a stroke or be struck down with cancer? The Lord's Prayer tells me: Ask God for what you need now. Our daily bread. That's good enough.

I don't think of certain prayers as lucky charms or talismans. You don't have to pick the right one or it won't work, as though prayer were a heavenly doctor's prescription: "Repeat the 23rd Psalm three times daily for stress" or "Take four Lord's Prayers for loneliness." It's not a question of what will get God's attention. As Jesus pointed out in Matthew, "Your Father knows what you need before you ask him." What matters is finding words that get *our* attention, that will focus us. The Lord's Prayer might be the only praying words you've ever known. Good. Use them.

Remember back in 2002 when the DC area was terrified by the Beltway Sniper? Ten people were killed and several wounded in a three-week period, all of them in the Maryland, Virginia and DC area. The killings were so random, usually with one bullet, often in parking lots and filling stations, that parents refused to send their kids to school. People were jumpy just filling their gas tanks. Truckers who came through the area were sending bulletins on their CB radios, looking first for what was said to be a white van and then more specifically a blue Chevy Caprice with New Jersey license plates.

Of course people were praying. Ron Lautz, a trucker from Ludlow, Kentucky, was one of them. He hadn't been much of a believer until his only son, Ron, was dying of multiple sclerosis. One October day, between his runs in his 18-wheeler, Ron visited his son at the nursing home. The boy was sitting on the edge of his bed, hands raised over his head, praising the Lord. For more than a year he hadn't been able to sit up on his own.

"I'm leaving here," the son said. "Someone's coming through that door tonight to take me home." He looked hard at his father. "Dad, I don't want to be up in heaven waiting for you and you don't make it. I want you to go over to my church right now and give your life to the Lord."

Ron did exactly that and gave his life to the Lord. His son didn't last the night, but Ron was a changed man. I don't know how a mom or dad could ever bear the pain of losing a child, let alone get out of bed in the morning. I can only admire their faith all the more. Ron got active in church, headed the men's fellowship, led retreats, was on the Sunday school board. And he never started a run without kneeling by the bed at the rear of his eighteen-wheeler cab and praying.

In those days of terror, with frequent trips through the DC area, Ron wondered what he could do. "I got to thinking about what I'd learned in church," he wrote, "how a bunch of people praying together can be more powerful than a person praying alone." What if he got on his CB to see if a few drivers wanted to pull off the road to pray with him?

He pressed the button on his microphone and said if anyone wanted to pray about the Beltway Sniper, Ron would meet them in half an hour at the eastbound sixty-six-mile-marker rest area of I-70.

One trucker answered right away, then another and another. Ron hadn't gone five miles before a line of trucks formed, some coming from behind, others up ahead. The line stretched for miles. It was getting dark when they pulled into the rest area. There must have been fifty rigs there. Everybody got out of their cabs and stood in a circle, holding hands, sixty or seventy of them, including some wives and children.

"Let us pray," Ron said. "Anyone who feels like it can start." He said the first one to speak up was a kid maybe ten years old, standing to his left. The boy bowed his head and prayed, "Our Father, who art in heaven..." They went around the circle. Some prayed their own words. Others repeated the Lord's Prayer. One phrase seemed particularly applicable: "Deliver us from evil." What could be more evil than this random violence?

Ten days later Ron was making his run through the DC area again, headed westbound on I-70. At the rest stop at the thirty-nine-mile marker near Myersville, Maryland, only a few miles from where everyone had gathered in a circle and prayed, the blue Chevy Caprice with New Jersey plates was spotted. Ron's eighteen-wheeler blocked the exit and the Beltway Sniper was caught and arrested—two men as it turned out. That was the headline in the next day's paper and on TV. I like the story of the truckers praying the Lord's Prayer at the sixty-six-mile marker even more. It's one of those rest-of-the-story moments you probably won't see on the news.

Fear was what gripped the nation and everybody in that Beltway area for those three weeks. Fear tends to feed on itself. When you're with people who are constantly looking over their shoulders, you start doing the same. Fear, as has often been pointed out, is love's opposite. Not hate, fear. Fear is what blocks you from loving someone, fear of being ridiculed, fear of rejection, fear of failure, fear of the unknown. Fear of dying can be so paralyzing that all faith disappears. When I was in the hospital getting ready for heart surgery, fear was what blocked me. "There is no fear in love, but perfect love casts out fear," the Bible says in 1 John 4:18 (RSV). How do you find that love when you're in a terrifying situation?

Toni Sexton and her husband, Rickey, were a sweet couple living in Wytheville, Virginia. I say "were" because Rickey is surely no longer with us. When we ran their story a dozen years ago he was wheelchair-bound from ALS—Lou Gehrig's disease—and as I knew only too well, having just lost one of my best friends to ALS, its progress is sure and devastating. But what I also knew from my friend was how precious those few last years could be.

Rickey had been a construction leader for the Virginia Department of Transportation, full of energy, always willing to help a neighbor. Three years after he was diagnosed, his muscles had wasted away. He'd stopped working. He lost his voice. Confined to a wheelchair, he could only nod his head and use his fingers a little. When he wanted to communicate to Toni, he spelled out the message and she interpreted it.

When he was well, Rickey made "power bands" for his friends, little leather bracelets knotted with colored beads. Each one was symbolic, a green bead for spiritual growth, yellow for heavenly glory, white for trust and forgiveness. After he got sick, his brother-in-law made them for him. He'd give them to his many visitors.

That April day Toni was headed to the mailbox. A car came screeching around the bend, turned into the driveway and skidded to a stop. A couple jumped out and ran towards her. The man had long, messy hair, wore faded jeans and a ripped T-shirt. The woman, a few years younger, probably in her twenties, had a pretty face and curly brown hair. Toni froze in her tracks. Both of them were carrying pistols.

"Get in the house!" the man yelled. He pushed Toni forward, slammed the door behind them, and ran into the living room, pulling down the blinds. The girl trained her gun on Toni. "Don't try anything," she said. A police cruiser tore down the road, siren blaring.

The man stared at Rickey in his wheelchair. "What's the matter with him?" he asked.

"He's got Lou Gehrig's disease," Toni explained. "He can't move anything but his fingers."

The man's name was Dennis and the girl's Angel. They stared out between the blinds. "There's cops everywhere!" Dennis said. More squad cars had pulled up and police swarmed around the house. "What are we going to do?" Angel asked. The two of them pushed furniture in front of the doors and covered all the windows.

"You got any drugs in this house?" Dennis demanded, waving his gun.

Toni went to get some of Rickey's muscle relaxants from the medicine cabinet in the bathroom. Dennis snatched the bottle from her and popped a few pills in his mouth, then tossed the bottle to the girl. Toni was swept by a fearful wave of recognition. She realized she'd seen them on the news. They'd assaulted two police officers and stolen their guns. The police were hunting them in two states.

She looked to her husband. Rickey spelled out something with his fingers: "Give them power bands."

The couple was dangerous, waving their guns around, high on pills. What would power bands do? But Rickey insisted. Toni dug them out of the bag in his wheelchair. She held out the bracelets.

"What's this?" Dennis snapped.

"A power band." She held out one for the girl, who put it on.

"What do the colors mean?" she asked.

Toni explained.

"Nobody ever gave me nothing before," Dennis said.

The day wore on. Angel clicked on the TV. Toni discovered that she was on the news. She made some Spam sandwiches. Dennis paced the front room, smoking. The phone rang. He barked at hostage negotiators. He slammed down the phone. They took more of Rickey's pills. There was tense silence.

Then Angel said in almost a whisper, "Would you do me a favor, ma'am? My mama used to read me the Lord's Prayer before I went to sleep at night. If you have a Bible, I sure would appreciate it."

Rickey nodded. Toni took the Bible from the shelf. Even though she knew the words well she found it comforting to read them and feel the weight of the book in her hands. "Thy kingdom come, thy will be done, on earth as it is in heaven." When she finished there was a longer silence, different this time.

"We're not going to get out of here alive," Dennis said. "We'll kill ourselves before we give up."

Rickey started spelling another message. Toni interpreted it out loud: "Please don't hurt yourselves. God loves you. I love you. God will get you through this. Trust him."

Nine hours had passed since Toni went to get the mail. Angel slumped at the kitchen table. Dennis's head dropped on his chest and he passed out. Toni leaned over and took Rickey's hand. He pressed it firmly. Then Angel got up, went to the phone and called the police. "We're ready to give up," she said. The siege ended without a shot being fired. "It was Rickey. He was the one who calmed them down and saved us," Toni said. Rickey, his power bands and a timeless prayer.

◆ ◆ ◆

Each phrase of the Lord's Prayer is worthy of a book, but the one that catches me, the hardest to live by and accept is "Thy will be done." For me, it only comes after a battle of wills, that point of surrender. You can't really be helped by anyone unless you acknowledge your need. I can get so defensive when I hear criticism that I'm unable to listen to the good in the critique. Same thing happens spiritually. If God knows what I need better than I know myself, why put up so much resistance? The old adage (not to be found anywhere in the Bible) "God helps those who help themselves" is true...until it's not true. We can sail through a dozen trials until we hit a wall. God's right there to lend a hand but usually we're so stubborn—or at least I am—that we're not willing to reach out and grasp it. We get so used to punching the wall, our hands balled into fists, that we don't know how to relax and accept the helping hand.

Have you ever watched someone parallel park? I can look out from my bedroom window down to the street below, a God's-eye view. I'll see a car pull out, a car behind waiting to take its place. The driver will check to see if there's enough room. "You've got at least a foot at either end," I want to shout. I watch the driver pull forward and back up, turning the steering wheel. Some drivers are great at it. Others are miserable even with plenty of extra space, rolling up over the curb, bumping the car in front. From my exalted position I can see exactly what they need to do. "Turn now!" I've been known to say. If they'd only listen. If they'd only hear. I suspect I'm often like those hapless drivers.

"It's good to remember that not even the Master Shepherd can lead if the sheep have not this trust and insist on running ahead of him or taking side paths or just stubbornly refusing to follow him," wrote Catherine Marshall in her *Guideposts* story "The Prayer of Relinquishment."

So when do we say "Thy will be done?" When to relinquish? Apparently all the time. At least if we follow the guidance of the Lord's Prayer. It's there up towards the front of the prayer: "Thy kingdom come, thy will be done, on earth as it is in heaven."

Usually when people refer to this powerful phrase, they mention Jesus in the Garden of Gethsemane on the night before his Crucifixion. He knew what was ahead and dreaded it. The fear must have been palpable, the horror immense. He didn't say "Thy will be done" right away. First he prayed, "Father, if you are willing, remove this cup from me." Then he exclaimed: "Yet not my will but yours be done." If he had to struggle with it, should we be surprised that we do too? Asking is a part of prayer. All that talk. But then give up when you need to give up. I've never been able to get there without a lot of work.

Catherine Marshall was married to longtime *Guideposts* editor Len LeSourd. She died in 1983, just about the time I started writing for *Guideposts*, so I never knew her personally but from all accounts she was a very demanding person, setting high standards for herself. It's what makes her a compelling writer. Her book about her first husband, Senate chaplain Peter Marshall, *A Man Called Peter*, was an instant bestseller and her novel *Christy* a perennial favorite, but the book I found most helpful was a slim volume about her day-to-day challenges of faith, *Adventures in Prayer*. She made no claims about prayer without testing them firsthand and tells her own powerful story about getting to "Thy will be done."

As a young woman she was bedridden with what she called "a widespread lung infection." No specialist could help her. No drug could cure her. Neither did her faith make a difference. "Persistent prayer," she wrote, "using all the faith I could muster, had resulted in nothing. I was still in bed full-time."

Then one afternoon she received a pamphlet about a missionary who had been an invalid for eight years. The woman had prayed and prayed that God would make her well. After all, if she were well she would be able to better do God's work. Nothing doing. Finally, all worn out, she prayed, "All right. I give up. If you want me to be an invalid, that's your business. Anyway, I want you even more than I want health. You decide." In two weeks the woman was out of bed, completely well.

None of this made sense to Catherine. Until she came to her own point of abject acceptance. She'd prayed and prayed with no answer. "I'm tired of asking," she finally said. "I'm beaten through, God. You decide what you want for me." Tears flowed. She had no faith anymore, at least not faith as she understood it. She expected nothing. And the result?

"It was as if I had touched a button that opened windows in heaven," she wrote, "as if some dynamo of heavenly power began flowing. Within a few hours I had experienced the presence of the living Christ in a way that wiped away all doubt and revolutionized my life. From that moment my recovery began.

"Through this incident and others that followed, God was trying to teach me something important about prayer. Gradually, I saw that a demanding spirit, with self-will as its rudder, blocks prayer. I understood that the reason for this is that God absolutely refuses to violate our free will; that, therefore, unless self-will is voluntarily given up, even God cannot move to answer prayer."

This is the hardest kind of faith to have because, as Catherine acknowledges, it involves a giving up of faith. A giving up of everything. In my own prayers it's where I land at two or three o'clock in the morning after I've failed at everything else. "Thy will be done" is a struggle. I can say it about relationships or even health easier than I can ever say it about something financial. God might know something about healing a broken heart or shrinking a nasty tumor, but what does he know about the S&P 500 or the check that's about to bounce? What does he know about the job market? What does he understand about adjustable rate mortgages and IRAs? I once interviewed a man who claimed that losing his dream house to foreclosure was the best thing that had happened to him. "I learned to trust God more than ever," he said. All I could think was, would I feel the same way?

"Faith is a gift but we can ask for it," Fulton Oursler, author of *The Greatest Story Ever Told*, wrote in *Guideposts* many years ago. Prayer is the asking. Bow your head and say the Lord's Prayer. Sing it in a crowded church, say it to yourself in the car on your way to work, run through the checklist of all it covers. It's like the Pledge of Allegiance or "The Star-Spangled Banner," repeated so often that you can forget how powerful it is. Say it in a time of need and you'll discover your faith anew.

The Lord's Prayer is so simple you can memorize the words in an hour. And you can spend the rest of your life learning how to live it.

## CHAPTER FIVE

# Praying for Forgiveness

*"I blew it, God."*

M y brother, Howard, was the first to call me on it. "You still haven't forgiven Dad," he said.

Dad had died and we'd mourned him with honest eulogies of all the good he'd given us. We counted ourselves lucky to have had such a father. Why bring up ancient history now? "Sure, I've forgiven him," I blithely told Howard. I could remember exactly when I'd done it eighteen years earlier, shedding the hurt like a eucalyptus tree shedding its old bark. It was all gone. Water under the bridge, as they say.

Then I paused and thought harder. Howard was right. My resentment was still there. Yes, I had forgiven Dad but I needed to go back and do it again. Forgiveness is like that. We need to do it all the time. Consciously, deliberately, jumping right back in the same murky waters until they become clear. To forgive and forget? Easier said than done and impossible without invoking a higher power. I wouldn't even try.

Corrie ten Boom knew a lot about forgiveness and had a lot to forgive. During World War II she and her sister Betsie had concealed Jews from the Nazis in their home in Holland. They were arrested and sent to the concentration camp at Ravensbrück, where Betsie died. A passionate Christian before the war, Corrie felt compelled in its aftermath to return to Germany to spread the message of forgiveness. It was the only way to heal from the horrors of the past, the only way she could possibly recover. "When we confess our sins," she often said, "God casts them into the deepest ocean forever."

In those brutal postwar days Germany was still a bombed-out, bitter, occupied land. Corrie had just given a talk in a church basement when a balding heavyset man in a gray overcoat came up to her, a hat clutched between his hands. "There were never questions after a talk in Germany in 1947," she wrote. "People stood up in silence, in silence collected their wraps, in silence left the room."

A look at this man's face immediately took her back to Ravensbrück, where he'd worn a blue uniform and a visored cap. She could see the huge room there with its harsh lights, the pathetic pile of dresses and shoes in the center on the floor and the shame of walking naked past him. She could picture her sister's frail form, the ribs sharp beneath the parchment skin. He had been a guard at the camp, a leather crop swinging from his belt.

Now he stood in front of her and thrust out his hand. "A fine message, fräulein," he said. "How good it is to know that, as you say, all our sins are at the bottom of the sea."

Corrie pretended to look for something in her purse. Here, she had just given a talk on forgiveness and she couldn't begin to forgive this man who had been one of her captors. Her blood seemed to freeze. "You mentioned Ravensbrück," he went on. "I was a guard there. But since that time I have become a Christian. I know that God has forgiven me for the cruel things I did there, but I would like to hear it from your lips, as well." He extended the hand again. "Will you forgive me?"

Anyone who has ever spoken to a group about some laudatory aspect of faith will be familiar with a moment like this. You've just said, "We should do..." or "God wants us to..." and you're suddenly asked to put into the practice the very virtue you've extolled. You want to squirm right out of it. You want to exclaim, "I didn't mean a situation like *this*, God," but there you are on the spot.

Two things I find very helpful about Corrie's depiction of forgiveness: One, you can't wait for the good feelings to come. You often have to act before you feel anything. "Forgiveness is an act of will," she wrote, "and the will can function regardless of the temperature of the heart."

"Jesus, help me," she prayed silently in that church basement. Woodenly, mechanically, she thrust her hand into the guard's outstretched hand. Only then did any healing warmth race through her. "I forgive you, brother," she could honestly say. They grasped each other's hands, the former guard and the former prisoner. It was done.

And her second point: Just because you have managed to forgive someone for some unspeakable wrong doesn't mean forgiveness is

all over. Corrie described another incident in which she had to forgive, a betrayal by friends she knew and loved. She was seething. She
acted against her feelings, proclaimed her forgiveness and a measure
of peace came. Done, she thought. But she awoke in the middle of
the next night, still rehashing the whole affair. How dare they! What
terrible behavior and from people she considered her dearest friends!
She sat up and switched on the light. "Father, I thought it was all
forgiven. Please help me do it again!" And again.

A pastor gave her a helpful analogy. Think of a bell in a church
tower. You pull on a rope and let go, the bell keeps ringing and ringing. Ding, dong, ding, dong. Slower and slower until it finally stops.
"When we forgive someone," he said, "we take our hand off the rope.
But if we've been tugging at our grievances for a long time, we mustn't
be surprised if the old angry thoughts keep coming for a while."

Working an old grievance can be a guilty pleasure, self-justification
a repeating refrain in our heads. Talk about a clanging bell. Our hurts
can so define us that letting them go is like erasing our personalities,
a frightening prospect. I used to think forgiveness would come easier
as I grew older. I'm not so sure now. Emotional pain can magnify with
age when left unattended. Not long ago I listened in wonder as my
colleague John Sherrill declared he needed to see a therapist because
his new pastor, a woman, brought up some painful memories from
childhood. "I found myself resenting her in a way that had nothing to
do with her. It all went back to my own mother," he said. "She was a
strong domineering woman and I needed to forgive some things she
had done." This from a man in his mid-eighties.

A forgiving spirit is a lasting grace but prayers of forgiveness are meant to be said again and again. Not for nothing is it part of the Lord's Prayer. *Forgive us our sins as we forgive those who sin against us.* John Sherrill's best friend from childhood, Van Varner, was the editor-in-chief who hired me at *Guideposts.* He had his own poignant example of learning how to understand and let go of the past when he too was in his eighties.

Van was a warm, courtly, charming Kentuckian who spent most of his life in New York City. He loved old movies, Broadway shows, walking his dog in Central Park and betting on the horses, having grown up in horse country. Impeccably dressed and urbane, he had an impish sense of humor and a way with puns. We met first through his godson Ty, a college classmate of mine. "Blessed be the Ty that binds," Van said the first time I met him. I had just submitted my first story to the magazine. "No, this story isn't quite right for us," he said, "but you should keep trying." As for the Ty/tie pun, it took me another ten years to figure that one out.

I adored Van. We all did. He was a marvelous teacher and editor. "The tears should be in the eyes of the reader," he often said, drawing a penciled line through any sentences on my drafts that were overwrought or too purple. Plain prose was the best way to tell a story. Don't have your subjects weep buckets of tears. Don't signal too much. If you've told a good story well, your readers will feel it.

He claimed he never cried over a story. He only wept singing "My Old Kentucky Home" at the start of the Kentucky Derby, which he generally watched by himself in his apartment on television, perhaps for that reason. There were hurts buried deep in his past that those who knew him could only guess at.

Van was the middle of three boys reared in Louisville. When he was five his parents divorced. Van prayed fervently for his parents to get back together. He prayed for them to love each other. He loved his father and was sure his mother still did too. Whatever had happened between them could be undone, couldn't it? His father sent the boys postcards almost every day, met them after school and was always present for Sunday dinner. Later his mother remarried, unhappily as it turned out, and the family moved to upstate New York. Van's prayers were never answered. He couldn't quite forgive God and couldn't quite give up hope for a rewrite to a story long finished.

None of this were we wholly aware of until Van, deep in his retirement, sent in a remarkable story of his own. (Tears in the eyes of this reader.)

Years ago, when his mother died, she had left behind an envelope that said: "Letters of Importance from Joe W. Varner." Van put the envelope in a safe-deposit box and for nearly half a century never looked inside. The memory of his parents' divorce was too painful. Why risk being hurt all over again? Every time he saw the envelope in the safe-deposit box he left it alone. "You figure that by the time you reach my point in life," he wrote, "things are what they are."

Then one day on a visit to the bank, he slipped off the rubber band on the yellowed envelope and finally looked inside. They weren't legal documents, as he'd assumed, but love letters his father had written *after* the divorce, always addressed "Dearest Mary Milam."

His mother had even saved a telegram his father had sent shortly before her remarriage: "IF NOT YET TOO LATE FOR YOU TO RECONSIDER..." His father frequently mentioned Van and his brothers. He was contrite and full of apologies. "You have been hurt...You have and do come first always in my heart."

Van had a new understanding of his parents. The bittersweet proof was in his hands. "They loved each other supremely," he wrote. "Their love was not perfect, as I had so believed when I was a boy. No, not ever that. But, oh, how human, and in its own imperfect human way, how lasting." After decades Van could finally let go. He could forgive God and his own expectations. He could see how his childhood prayer had been answered after all.

As an editor Van would urge us to look for stories that weren't simply front-page, dramatic, made-for-TV-movie situations. We all can imagine how hard it must be to forgive a loved one's killer face-to-face. We can read about it and admire the faith of a saintly Corrie ten Boom and say to ourselves, "I don't know if I could do that." But it can be just as hard to forgive—and just as admirable—in our day-to-day struggles. Think of the grudges we nurse and cling to long after their expiration date. The sister we stopped speaking to when she took the heirloom tea service out of the dining room right after Mom's death. The colleague who poisons the workplace because of jealousy. The husband who bitterly resents the demands of his wife's career yet says nothing to her about it. The child whose prayer never seemed answered. Simmering resentments are deadly barriers to a godly life.

"When you are offering your gift at the altar, if you remember that your brother or sister has something against you, leave your gift there before the altar and go, first to be reconciled to your brother or sister and then come and offer your gift," Jesus said (Matthew 5:23–24, RSV). We can't be reconciled to God if we're not reconciled to each other and to our loved ones. Doing that can take a big gesture, something extravagant and bold. You're trying to rewrite a script that has gone awry, redoing a story. I think of something Beatriz Sandoval—or B, as her friends and siblings call her—did when she wanted to reconnect with her mother after a deep chill. I wish I could show you the picture of her we ran in the magazine, a beautiful dark-haired woman surrounded by flowers—"a fragrant offering," to use Paul's words for it.

B is from a large Latino family in Southern California. She and her mother had had a rocky relationship for years. She remembered being teased as a child for being chubby and wearing glasses. "You'll never get a boyfriend the way you look," relatives would say—and her own mother wouldn't defend her. She hated that. Moreover, she resented being at her mom's beck and call as a girl. No matter how hard she worked she felt she could never earn her mom's approval. Even after she moved out of the house and became successful in her career, B never made peace with her mom. After one bad argument, B told her mom that she never wanted to talk to her again. And for five years she didn't.

"You should call your mom sometime," her husband said. B brushed off his suggestion. She wasn't about to back down. If her mom was being stubborn, she could be stubborn too. They were alike in that.

Then B's sister Leticia announced that she was getting married and wanted B to be the maid of honor. B was thrilled. She could picture the shower she would put on and wanted to do all she could to make her sister's wedding unforgettable.

One problem: Her mother would have to be included in all the events and the silence between the two of them would be unbearable. Already the family held separate holiday gatherings so that B and her mom wouldn't have to be in the same room. B could see how their feud had the potential of dividing the entire family. She should put an end to it. But how would she reverse things? How could she find words to express everything she felt?

"Okay, Lord," she prayed, "I know what I need to do, but I can't do it without you. I'm really going to need your help with this one."

One day on her way to work, B stopped at a florist's. Her mom loved flowers. B held the cooler door open, trying to choose between a red bouquet, a pink bouquet and a white bouquet. Suddenly with a sweep of her arm she grabbed every bouquet from the cooler and carried them to the counter. Eight dozen roses. She paid quickly and hustled to the car. "This is crazy," she thought, but it was what she needed to do.

B pulled into her mother's driveway. She saw her mother standing in the garage. Was her mother crying? B gathered the bouquets in her shaking hands and stepped out of the car.

Her mother *was* crying, her proud, stoic, stubborn mom. For the first time B realized how the separation had hurt her mom.

B rushed to the garage, set the flowers down and took her mom in her arms. "You don't have to cry, Mom. I'm here now," she said.

"*Mi hija*," she repeated over and over. "My daughter, my beautiful daughter."

"Let's not talk about it, Mom," B said, forcing back her own tears. "What do you think?" She pointed to the flowers. "Did I get enough?" They both laughed and went inside to find vases.

The flowers expressed what B couldn't possibly have said with words. She felt relief, exhaustion, excitement and peace rush through her. She had done something that she had desperately needed to do for a long time. Not just for those five years of angry silence but for a lifetime of pent-up resentment. Eight bouquets to express her love. Who was at fault? They both were. B could see that now. "Forgiving and being forgiven are two names for the same thing," said C. S. Lewis. They work in tandem.

"Let all bitterness and wrath and anger and clamor and slander be put away from you, along with all malice," Paul wrote in his letter to the Ephesians (4:31–32, KJV). "Be kind to one another, tenderhearted, forgiving one another as God in Christ forgave you." In one wild beautiful generous gesture, B said that with flowers. Don't think for a minute that those roses were not also a prayer.

◆ ◆ ◆

Not forgiving, not praying for forgiveness, not letting go, can be dangerous not only to your spiritual well being but also to your physical health. Anger turned inward is poisonous. Old wounds left untreated fester. One of the things I find freeing about praying the Psalms is the expression of anger. The psalmist speaks honestly about evil, entreating God in Psalm 139, "Do I not hate them that hate thee, O Lord? Am I not grieved with those that rise up against thee? I hate them with a perfect hatred. I count them my enemies." Before you can forgive your enemies you have to know who they are.

Carolyn Maull McKinstry was afraid something terrible would happen if she got too close to other people, even her husband and her two young daughters, so she barely talked to anyone. She found herself drinking in the middle of the day. She didn't sleep. She picked at her food. She lost weight. Her hands were always breaking out in rashes. She was in a state of constant misery and didn't know why.

Her husband, Jerome, walked in on her in their Atlanta home when she was on the phone to a suicide hotline. "I just wanted someone to talk to," she told him. "I was lonely." Jerome insisted she speak to their doctor and she ended up in a psychologist's waiting room.

Carolyn had grown up in Birmingham, Alabama, at the height of the civil rights struggles. The city had been nicknamed Bombingham because of all the bombs that had destroyed black homes, businesses and churches. Her father had done his best to shelter his family from the troubles. Strict rules were observed, the politics of desegregation never discussed. Carolyn was not allowed to go anywhere without being escorted by one of her brothers. Church was the only place she could go alone.

The family went to Sixteenth Street Baptist Church downtown. Carolyn was baptized there at age thirteen, and remembered staring at the tender face of Jesus in the stained-glass window after her pastor lifted her from the water. "It seemed as if he were telling me, 'I'm here, watching over you.'" She'd been happy, trusting, carefree, not constantly afraid like she was now.

The psychologist asked her about her symptoms, the sleepless nights, the drinking during the day. Finally he said, "What you're dealing with is depression. It's treatable but you won't survive if you keep on like this.

"I can't help but think there's something, maybe in your past, you need to let go of. We need to figure out what's bothering you."

Something in her past? Carolyn had tried not to dwell on it, but it would never go away. She would never forget.

She drove home from the doctor's and took down a box of old things from her closet. On the top was the Bible her parents had given her when she was baptized. She'd had it with her on that terrible day she had never been able to forget: September 15, 1963, Youth Sunday.

She'd been laughing with her friends in the restroom at the church—Cynthia, Denise, Addie and Carole. She was the Sunday school secretary and had to go upstairs to hand in her attendance and offering report by 10:30. When she was in the office the phone rang. She held the receiver up to her ear. A man's voice said, "Three minutes," then hung up. What was that about? She still needed to collect the report from the adult classes. She walked into the sanctuary, toward the stained-glass image of Jesus.

*Boom!* The floor swayed. Glass fell at her feet. Someone shouted, "Hit the floor!" She dropped flat on the ground. There was a stampede of feet. Sirens. She had to get out. She looked up and saw a hole in the stained-glass window where Jesus' face had been.

The streets were filled with people screaming and crying. She found her father behind a police barricade. They drove home in silence, too scared to talk. Why would anyone bomb their church?

That afternoon their phone rang at home. Carolyn remembered her mother answering it, listening, then hanging up, her face filled with sorrow. There were four girls in the restroom who never made it out. Carolyn's four friends. Dead.

That night Carolyn burrowed deep under the covers, but it was hours before she was able to sleep. Why did people want to kill her congregation, her friends? Why would they bomb a house of God? And that mysterious phone call, was that a warning? Could she have done anything? The world would never seem safe again. A terrible emptiness opened up inside. It haunted her, through high school, college, her marriage. No one had ever asked her what she thought. She hadn't gone to the funeral because she wanted to remember her friends as she'd last seen them, in the restroom laughing in front of the mirror. What she really wanted was for their killers to suffer. She wanted them to feel as much pain as she did.

Now she sat with her old Bible. "God," she prayed, "I am in so much pain. Please fix my body. Take away my craving for alcohol. Please touch me with your healing." She felt the weight of the Bible in her hands. It fell open. There was an old church bulletin tucked inside. September 15, 1963, the day of the bombing. Youth Sunday.

She read through the hymn selections and the names of the people who were to give the prayers. Then she saw the pastor's sermon title, "A Love That Forgives." The Scripture text was Luke 23:24. Carolyn turned to the passage: "Father, forgive them, for they know not what they do."

Tears streamed down her cheeks. She thought of that stained-glass window of Jesus reaching out to her. He was still doing it, all these years later, years that she'd carried a terrible burden inside. "Forgive me, Lord, for not coming to you before now," she prayed, "for not trusting you." She could picture the bombers and their fear. She could understand the enemy. *Forgive them as you have forgiven me.* She could feel the hardness in her heart melting, the anger and bitterness flowing from her.

Carolyn's depression didn't disappear overnight but she'd taken the first step. Like Corrie ten Boom, she would have to return to prayer again and again. Forgiving wasn't something she could do on her own. She kept seeing the psychologist, kept growing in her faith. She and Jerome moved back to Birmingham and became members of Sixteenth Street Baptist Church. Eventually she went to divinity school so she could spread her message.

"The church holds a special status in the history of the civil rights movement," she wrote, "a symbol of faith and hope for all who enter its doors. For me it will always be a reminder of God's infinite grace and love for all his children, and how we are given that love in order to forgive what seems unforgivable and release our burdens to him."

◆ ◆ ◆

Every Sunday in our church we say a communal prayer of confession that comes right out of the Book of Common Prayer: "Most merciful

God, we confess that we have sinned against you in thought, word and deed, by what we have done and by what we have left undone..." I especially like that phrase "by what we have left undone," a reminder of the dangers of spiritual sloth, a goad to do something. Faith requires giving up, letting go. And yet it is anything but passive. It is work. Asking for forgiveness means taking a moral and emotional inventory. Not burying the least attractive parts of ourselves but bringing them to light. That seems so counterintuitive. I would rather consider myself Mr. Super Nice Guy rather than admit to those moments when I blew it. Quite frankly if it weren't on the weekly agenda at church I would probably skip it. And yet how would I move forward in faith if I didn't look for those things "done" and "left undone" and let them go?

I'm reminded of a liturgical gesture I've seen in some worship services, particularly with my Catholic friends, when the priest raps at his chest with his fist. What a great way to express the pain. "I hurt you, God, and I have hurt myself. Forgive me."

Confession seems the most private of moments, and yet there is wisdom in a community praying for forgiveness together. A whole community suffers when it doesn't forgive. "Now if anyone has caused pain, he has caused it not to me, but in some measure—not to put it too severely—to all of you," Paul wrote in his second letter to the Corinthians. "For such a one, this punishment by the majority is enough, so you should rather turn to forgive and comfort him, or he may be overwhelmed by excessive sorrow. So I beg you to reaffirm your love for him." One of the most extraordinary recent examples of communal forgiveness was in an Amish community after the killing and wounding of ten schoolgirls. Some in the media criticized them for their quickness to offer forgiveness—as though it weren't authentic or didn't fully acknowledge the evil—but it was so obviously at the heart of what knit them together. They lived by it.

Let me get back to that conversation I had with my brother, Howard.

Our dad was not perfect. He had his demons. I've already hinted at them, but that doesn't make it any easier to write about them. Maybe if I first emphasized Dad's deep faith and his heartbreakingly honest prayers, I've told myself, you could read this in the forgiving spirit in which it's meant. But it took me a long while to understand it myself. "God is not always choosy about the vessels of his grace," wrote the Canadian writer Robertson Davies, a line I underlined and circled when I first read it.

The biggest difficulty I had with my dad was his drinking. If he had too much, as he often did in my late teens and twenties, he didn't become more jovial or jolly. He became less than himself. His natural sentimentality turned mawkish. His deep sensitivity veered into self-pity. His extraordinary spirituality seemed gone.

As children naturally seek to understand their parents, I looked for clues. I asked my closest minister/therapist friend, Rick Thyne. We talked about all my dad's strengths. "Your father would drop everything to help someone," Rick said.

I knew he would. Yet how could a man be so spiritual and good and generous but also unable to cut back on the cocktails when he was, to use my brother-in-law's phrase, "overserved?"

Dad was our faith mentor at home, an upright Presbyterian with deep roots. Mom taught Sunday school. Mom had a spiritual awakening at one of those famous Billy Graham crusades that transformed LA after World War II. But Dad was the reason we went to church. On Sunday mornings Dad was an usher, the gold embroidered cross on a burgundy background displayed on his suit-coat pocket. Dad served on the board of deacons, then the board of elders in our church long before Mom ever did (probably before women were allowed in those roles). I've known people who had problems with the concept of a heavenly father because of what their earthly fathers were like. Not me. Dad was a righteous man.

"Does he drink because of something that happened to him during the war?" I asked Rick. Was it some lingering response to the trauma that he had suffered in the submarine corps during World War II? Some late and long-running sequel to *The Best Years of Our Lives*, which I'd seen on TV as a kid?

"Do you think he's self-medicating for some post-traumatic stress?" I wondered.

Dad served on a submarine through two war patrols. Unlike other dads who never spoke of the war, he didn't hesitate to give us a vivid picture of what it was like — if we were listening. At the dinner table, he described what happened when his sub dove deep under some Japanese vessel searching for them, crawling at the bottom of the Pacific. "We could hear the depth charges dropping around us," he said. "We walked around in our socks and whispered as if the Japanese could hear us."

"What would happen if they found you?" we asked.

"They would take down the whole sub. That was the thing about the submarine corps. You all died or you all survived."

He took us to a museum to show us a submarine just like his. It was tiny. I would have been terrified to spend an hour, let alone months, on a boat like that. I didn't even like it with the hatch open and sunlight streaming in. He came back from the war rail-thin and jumpy, according to old letters, and he probably drank a lot. His whole generation drank a lot. But he wasn't rail-thin and jumpy when I was in my teens. Not externally at least.

Drinking as a response to some long-ago war trauma? I didn't completely buy it.

The conversation with Rick Thyne and my siblings and others went on for decades, as such conversations do. Rick happened to introduce me to the writings of M. Scott Peck, author of the wildly popular *The Road Less Traveled*. In a later book Peck wrote about alcoholism being a spiritual disease. Alcoholics, if my dad had been one—he would never have said he was—were often very spiritual people, Peck said. When they couldn't fulfill spiritual longings, they turned to drink as a substitute. Not for nothing was hard liquor called "spirits."

That made sense to me. Dad was comfortable in his faith, but sometimes he went to the wrong place for a spiritual fill-up.

Then there were glimpses we'd get of some lingering sadness, a story or two he'd tell at an unguarded and yes, lubricated moment. His mother had breast cancer when he was twelve years old, a double mastectomy in the late years of the Depression.

"I didn't see her for a whole summer," he said to me. "She went into the hospital and they didn't tell us why. I didn't know if she was going to live or going to die. Nobody said anything."

Imagine what that would be like for a sensitive kid like my dad. Like me.

My prayer for myself was to just let go of the whole thing. Drinking didn't get in the way of his work. It didn't seem to harm his health. It didn't bother Mom. It was under control—mostly. But it bothered me. I didn't enjoy him when he drank too much. It marred my image of who my father was. I didn't like being so judgmental of someone I loved and admired deeply. "Help me let it go, God," I could say, but I couldn't let it go. It gnawed at me. I wasn't able to sort the good Dad from the troubled one who drank and the drinking one threatened to overshadow our relationship. I couldn't forgive.

When I was in my late thirties, I had my own wake-up call. It was as though God was shaking me by the shoulders and saying, "Sure, you can forgive. Look for the big picture. See your dad the way I see him."

Carol and I lived in New York with our two sons. Mom and Dad were frequent visitors to our apartment. We loved seeing them. They were good grandparents. But whenever Dad came he needed a bottle of vodka and I could never bring myself to buy it for him. I would let him go to the liquor store. I cringe at the memory. It seems inhospitable, ungracious, unloving. I say now, "Rick, why didn't you give him a break? He was so good to you in so many ways. Why couldn't you be as generous?"

That spring we hit the roughest patch we ever had in our young family. Tim, age four, broke his femur in a tricycle accident at nursery school. Will, age seven, came down with the chicken pox a day later. Tim had to be in traction for twenty-seven days at the hospital. Will was sick at home. Carol and I were darting back and forth between the two places.

Mom came out for a week and was her helpful, upbeat self. Then she went home. She'd done more than her duty as mom, grandmother and mother-in-law.

In the midst of all this I was diagnosed with a tumor on my parotid gland. It had to come out. Soon. So while Tim was in traction at the hospital and Will was recovering from chicken pox, I had surgery. It was supposed to be an easy procedure, a quick recovery—or so the doctors said. But I came home after a night in the hospital in misery. Half the nerves in my face were bruised and unresponsive. I could only half smile, couldn't blink one eye or squint. Worse, I couldn't sleep but was groggy from the general anesthesia. How was I going to take care of a kid with chicken pox if I couldn't take care of myself? Carol was busy enough with Tim at the hospital.

Mom and Dad called me that night. "Hi," Dad said, "how are you?"

"Not so great," I said. I gave a synopsis, then hung up. Dad called back five minutes later. "I'm taking the night flight out, the red-eye," he said. "I'll be there in the morning."

First thing in the morning, with the dawn, Dad pulled up to our apartment, stepping out of a cab in his red sweater vest. I replayed the words my friend Rick Thyne had said to me years before. He was right. My dad would drop anything to help someone. He did the big things right. The drinking shrank back into proportion. Forgiveness came easy then. Didn't even have to try.

◆ ◆ ◆

But remember how I said forgiveness was something you had to go back and do again and again? Hence my conversation with Howard. He saw something and was calling me on it. I had to figure out what it was. Where was this new anger coming from? Why the resentment only months after Dad's funeral, a spiritual send-off that was as cleansing as anything I'd known? Hadn't I forgiven?

I realized it was a borrowed resentment, an unforgiving heart that came not just from Dad but also from my anger at alcoholism on my wife's side of the family. One of the great gifts of the twelve-step movement is the insistence on honesty, and now I had to be honest with myself. I was angry with my mother-in-law, even all these years after her death. *You need to forgive her too*, I thought.

Carol's mother's given name was Moon. She was a brilliant, charming, clever woman who did *The New York Times* crossword puzzle in ink—finished it by 9:00 AM—and could cook anything. Soft-shell crabs dipped in batter, sweetbreads for Carol's birthday, lobster with tons of butter, pecan pies at Thanksgiving. She was a voracious reader, going through books so fast she gave most of them away to the library because there was no room left on her shelves. Moon loved her dogs, coddling her pugs and addressing her German shepherds in German as though it were her native tongue.

She'd been a beauty in her youth, tall and blonde with blazing blue eyes and a strong chin. She was the queen of the annual pageant in the Mississippi River city where she grew up, and sometimes I wondered if that was part of the problem. All that attention before she was twenty, posing at civic events in her tiara, having her picture in the paper. It would have to be all downhill from there.

By the time I knew her she'd been divorced for a dozen years, although there was always some man in the picture enjoying her humor, her cooking and, truth be told, the chance to drink together. For by then my mother-in-law had a serious drinking problem, far worse than anything my dad ever had. The morning began with vodka. She'd drink it from a jam jar while she did the crossword, and the drinking continued throughout the day. There were times of day when Carol simply didn't call her.

This was always most noticeable in the fall when Moon wanted to know about our Christmas plans. As early as September she'd call and ask: "Tell me, what should I get the boys for Christmas? What do they want this year?"

Carol steeled herself for these conversations. She checked caller ID and looked at her watch—any time after five was hopeless. She wanted to be sure her mother was lucid. She didn't want to be disappointed again. "Okay, Mom," Carol would finally give in. She'd pick something off of Santa's list and send Moon a catalogue, the right page dog-eared with the perfect present circled in red.

The conversations continued intermittently all fall. "What was it that the boys wanted for Christmas?" There were other talks about

Christmas: Whose family would we be with, when, and what should we eat this year, turkey or roast beef? But it was the conversations about the boys' presents that were the hardest to take.

The final call always came a week or two before the twenty-fifth. Carol answered. Moon sighed. "Could you buy something for the boys and tell them it came from me? I'll send you a check later."

I wished I could have protected Carol from the despair she plunged into after this last conversation. I prayed I could relieve her sorrow. Sometimes I was tempted to say, "Don't do it. Don't buy them anything from your mom." What was a gift if it didn't involve some effort for the giver? Instead, Carol had to wonder if her mom really loved the boys; she could do so little for them when she was under the influence. Moon made promises but was too unwell to keep them. That realization didn't relieve the anguish. Dutifully, Carol wrapped up something for the boys from their grandmother and buried her pain.

Then the year the boys turned twelve and nine, Carol and her sisters gathered together, determined that their mother get some help. They organized an intervention. On an August morning at seven o'clock we arrived at Moon's house. We sat around her dining room table and asked her, as lovingly as possible, to go into a twenty-eight-day inpatient treatment facility. She listened to us with strained patience. The jam jar was full, the crossword was waiting. "All right," she sighed. "I'll go."

I can't fathom how hard this must have been. For a sixty-nine-year-old woman to leave her comfortable home, bid farewell to her dogs, her kitchen and her garden and live in a dormitory with total strangers, all going to mandatory lectures, AA meetings, group therapy and one-on-one sessions. Like a prison sentence. None of us had any hope the treatment would really work—this wasn't the first time we'd tried. But none of us could tolerate the status quo any longer.

Moon came out of the program looking great. She even managed to thank us. "I will never let that happen again," she promised. She went to meetings regularly. She started seeing a therapist. She talked about the changes she would make in her life. We were hopeful but wary, Carol wariest of all.

That fall there were none of the usual phone calls from Moon about what she would get the boys for Christmas. "It's just as well," I said. "She's got other things on her mind. She's working on her sobriety." If we had only known what was really wrong.

In November Moon collapsed at home with what seemed to be a massive stroke. She had no speech, little movement. It wasn't even clear if she recognized any of us at the hospital. Every day for ten days Carol was at her mother's bedside. At first there was some faint hope that she would recover. Then the doctors determined that the stroke had been caused by an aggressive cancer that riddled her body. All we could do was wait and make sure she was in no pain.

Moon died two days before Thanksgiving. At her burial service we gathered around her grave, all of us crying. It was hard not to ask ourselves a hundred what-ifs. What if we had done the intervention earlier? What if we had worked harder at getting her to give up drinking? Maybe she would have discovered the cancer sooner. Maybe we wouldn't be standing around a grave but celebrating birthdays and Thanksgivings and Christmases for many years to come.

An old family friend, another recovering alcoholic, held up a coin. "This was to commemorate Moon's first ninety days of sobriety. Nothing made her prouder."

Our mood that Christmas was muted. Carol was only going through the motions. She bought the presents, did the decorating, read the Christmas cards, sang the carols, but her heart wasn't in any of it. "You don't have to go to any parties this year," I told her. "Everybody will understand."

The packages piled up. Presents from relatives, from friends. Boxes from websites and catalogues where we'd shopped. We knew what was in those boxes. Something I ordered. Something Carol ordered. But one day a package arrived from a company that neither Carol nor I had ever heard of. "Do you know what's in here?" I asked. And why was it addressed to the boys and not to us? It was a big box.

I cut through the tape and dumped out all the Styrofoam worms. I put my hands in and pulled out a globe. A beautiful globe of the world. "Who's this from?" I asked Carol.

She fished out the order form. She looked and then turned away. It was from her mother. A Christmas present for the boys.

There is a story, surely apocryphal, about a Filipino peasant who claimed to have spoken to Jesus. The woman was passed along from parish to parish until finally the bishop interviewed her. Had she really seen Jesus? Could she really speak to the Lord? With an apparent attempt to trap her, the bishop said, "If you truly speak to Jesus, will you please ask Jesus what my sins are? He would know all about them. I've confessed them to him often enough."

A few weeks passed and the peasant woman came back to the bishop. "Did you speak to Jesus?" he asked.

"Yes," the woman replied.

"Did you ask him what my sins are?"

"Yes," she said. And then with the utter simplicity of the saint, she added, "He forgot."

Our sons got other presents that year. Lego astronauts, a baseball bat, football jerseys, a set of Narnia tapes, but nothing quite like the present from their grandmother Moon, who loved them and was finally able to express that love because she was at long last well.

No, I don't think I can ever forget. I'm not that holy. But I can forgive. And I have to, again and again. I can hear that bell Corrie ten Boom spoke of ringing and ringing. This can mean forgiving someone I've already forgiven or wasn't even the person I thought I was angry with. It can take me back to resentments I thought were long gone. Anger, particularly anger from childhood, has a way of lurking below the surface and when the waters get churned up, it can rise to the top. Watch out. Hurtful behavior from one person can remind you of other hurts. Just because you've buried the dead doesn't mean you've forgiven them.

"Thanks, Howard," I said. "I haven't completely forgiven Dad." Or Moon. The realization was enough. There were healing stories I could turn to. But I suspect if I live into my eighties, I'll still be at it like Van Varner and John Sherrill.

God knows there are ways I've hurt others. Forgiving is the only way to a clean slate.

## CHAPTER SIX

# Pray through a Crisis

———◆◇◆———

*"Nooooooooo!"*

The calls came when I was at lunch. I returned to the office to find my voice mail full of urgent messages from California. First from my older sister. She was breathless and in a hurry, jumping into her car to drive to the hospital in Long Beach. "Ricky," she said, "we need your help. There's been an accident. Mike was in a plane crash. Right at the airport. He's the only survivor. Five other guys died. He's being rushed to the ER. Please pray. Pray."

My mom was the next to leave a message: "Honey, I don't know if you heard but it's Mike. He was in a plane crash at the airport in Long Beach. I'm heading down there now. He survived. I don't know how he survived but it's very, very serious. We need your prayers. Poor Diane and the girls."

Diane called too. "Ricky, Mike's holding on, but we all need to pray. Please pray."

I listened to the messages with a sinking feeling. Mike is my younger sister Diane's husband. He's a big boisterous guy with bottlebrush blond hair, a loud voice, a louder laugh and thighs the size of tree trunks. His idea of fun was to ride his bike a hundred miles before breakfast on a Saturday morning. It was impossible to imagine that anyone so physically fit could be hurt. He was wired and funny and full of energy, always forwarding some e-mail about politics or faith or some combination of both. He worked hard running a small business and worked just as hard at his faith, filling up notebooks with Bible verses. He led grace at family dinners with a greeting that could be heard down the palm-lined block: "DEAR GOD..."

I felt so helpless. I wanted to be with my sister Diane and her three girls in the hospital waiting room, getting constant updates. I wanted to hug them, talk to them. I wanted to hear it straight from a straight-talking doctor coming out from the swinging ER doors. Was Mike going to survive? I needed to know exactly what the damage was. "Ricky, please pray." What else could I do? It was as though prayer was the only refuge of the helpless.

I returned calls. Got my older sister, Gioia, on the line. "What happened?"

"Mike and five other guys were on a business trip," Gioia said. "They took off from the airport in a small plane. It crashed right after takeoff. It's all over the news. The engine must have caught on fire. The plane was in flames. When they put the fire out, Mike was the only one alive."

How awful. Horrific. "Where are his burns?"

"All over."

What about brain damage, internal damage? What about his heart? What about his lungs? When would they know?

"Who was with him?" I asked.

"Guys he worked with, colleagues, friends," she said, "the pilot, the owner of the plane."

"*Ughhhhhhhh.*" I can't even put down the sound I made. "This is terrible."

"We've all got to pray. Please pray."

"Where's Mom?"

"She's in the car with me," Gioia said. "We're driving down there right now."

"Keep me posted," I said. "I'll pray." But what would my prayer be? All I could come up with was an awful groan. "No, God, *noooooooooo!* Don't let him die. Not Mike. Not with those other guys already dead." What an awful thing, a horrendous tragedy. I could barely take it in.

I put down the phone and rocked in my chair, leaning forward, hugging my stomach, trying to hold the pain in and hold back the sound. A month earlier, almost exactly a month earlier, Dad had died and we'd all been together. There are prayers for moments like that, prayers for a natural passing, prayers of mourning and loss. But there was no prayer for a moment like this except "*Noooooooooo!*" I couldn't find anything else.

I called Carol. "I have this feeling that Mike's going to make it," I said, wanting to reach for hope. Grasping at straws. "He's really strong. He's got a strong faith, a strong will to live." Who was I spinning things for? It didn't take away the pain I felt. "Nooooooooo!" went the prayer loop in my head.

How can an inner scream be much of a prayer? "You're a writer," I tell myself. "You're an editor. Can't you come up with fancier words for a prayer than that? Can't you articulate it?" But at that moment there was nothing else.

I prayed in stunned anger and fear. I called our sons to let them know: "A terrible thing has happened to your uncle Mike..." I e-mailed friends and texted them, widening the network, sounding just like my mom and sisters when they called me. "Pray, please pray," I said. That was all there was to do. The only possible response.

Prayer connected us those first twenty-four hours. All of us were desperately clinging to hope, the believing and non-believing, those of us praying fervently and those stumbling at prayer. I did some of both. I had to check in hour by hour for progress reports. I'm not the sort who can retreat to a mountaintop, unplug my connection with the world and devote myself to prayer. Not by a long shot.

Mike and Diane's friends gathered at the hospital. Many of them knew the other guys, the ones who hadn't survived. Their focus was on Mike, the sole survivor. He had to make it. I could picture the scene, the kids pretending to do homework in the orange plastic chairs, the parents whispering to each other.

Mike and Diane's minister showed up and led the group in prayer. The hospital served sandwiches. In a crisis it's easy to forget to eat. Night fell. Everybody left. Diane kissed her daughters good-bye and stayed at the hospital. My sister Gioia stayed with her, the two of them prepared for an all-night vigil.

The doctors worked on Mike all night. They gave him forty pints of blood and ran him through a battery of tests.

There is a litany of medical terms to describe a patient's state, putting into clinical language what is too terrible to describe: "The patient is in critical condition...serious condition...critical but stabilized." We were looking for words to tell us not only if Mike was going to survive but also in what state. Where were the burns? How bad were they? What bones were broken?

Around midnight my "Noooooooo!" changed to a "Please, God, please." The doctors had been feeding us small nuggets of information. There was no apparent brain damage. His heart, his kidneys and his liver were all right. There was hope for his lungs, even after all that noxious smoke. What a miracle. But second- and third-degree burns still covered a third of his body. Once he was stabilized he would have to go to a burn unit for the painful scrubbing of old scarred tissue and grafting of skin. He would be there for a very long time.

I felt greedy praying, "Please, please" in this terrible disaster. Five good men had been killed, leaving behind wives and children, empty desks, empty beds, empty offices. "Please, God, can't some good come from this? Can't there be one ray of hope? Don't give up on Mike."

After thirty-six hours it looked like Mike would survive. In what shape, with what capacities, it wasn't clear. But an ambulance could take him to the burn unit for the long struggle and painful treatment ahead. My "Noooooooo!" faded into a brief sense of relief and a moment of thankfulness but "Noooooooo!" had served its purpose, keeping me connected when I was feeling undone.

There's a tendency to whitewash God, to make the Lord into some cosmic Santa Claus, always jolly, perennially upbeat, never displeased, never angry. But when I'm angry, I'm not in the mood for a laughing Santa Claus. I need a God bigger than that, someone who can understand my pain, someone who can match the depth of my feelings. Let's not be so quick to diminish God's power or wrath. "O Lord, do not rebuke me in your anger, or discipline me in your wrath," are the sharp words of Psalm 6. "Be gracious to me, O Lord, for I am languishing. O Lord, heal me, for my bones are shaking with terror…I am weary with my moaning. Every night I flood my bed with tears. My eyes waste away because of grief."

"Noooooooo!" is the sound of my prayer when I turn to God in desperation. I don't look for him to smile at me with bland reassurance. The people I turn to when I really need help are big, passionate, caring, generous, knowledgeable about human frailty. They can match my anger, they understand my fears, they can love me when I'm at my most unlovable. They're right there with me when I'm "weary with my moaning" and my eyes "waste away because of grief." The same is true of the God who loves me and whom I love back, in spite of the worst.

"If I believe that he can love me, I must also believe that I can love him. If I do not believe I can love him, then I do not believe him who gave us the first commandment: 'Thou shalt love the Lord thy God with thy whole heart and thy whole mind and all thy strength and thy neighbor as thyself,'" wrote Thomas Merton. Loving God means being willing to shout to him "No!" Sometimes I think he's saying "Noooooooo!" right back with me.

◆ ◆ ◆

Marian and Chris Hammaren had one child, their daughter Caitlin, a nineteen-year-old sophomore at Virginia Tech. The Hammarens lived in upstate New York, an eight-hour drive from the campus, but Marian kept in touch with Caity by texting. In fact, that August day when the Hammarens dropped Caitlin off for freshman orientation, they weren't ten minutes north of Blacksburg when Marian got her first text: "I LOVE my room, Mom. And I know I'm going to love it here. Don't worry. XXC."

Caitlin was busy with wall-to-wall activities, prelaw classes, church, her job as a resident advisor, her sorority. "If you're too busy to call," Marian told her daughter, "just text me an OK. If you're too busy for that, just type an 'O.'" Caitlin laughed.

On the night of April 15, 2007, a nor'easter blew through the Hammarens' upstate town. "The radio's predicting floods," Marian texted her daughter. "Can you BELIEVE it?"

The Hammarens had to dig a trench that night to keep their house from flooding. Two hours later, they came inside, dried off and Marian checked her cell phone. Caity had left a message: "Let me know how it turns out! XOC."

"All's well," Marian typed back. "Dad has it under control. Love, hugs and kisses. Talk to you tomorrow."

There was no message the next morning, but that wasn't unusual. It was still early. Marian headed in to work where she is an occupational therapist. She'd just walked into her office when Chris called. "Turn on your computer. There's a problem at Virginia Tech." Then her cell rang. It was a classmate of Caitlin's. Had Marian heard from her? "No," Marian said. "What's going on?"

"I don't know," Caitlin's friend said. "But it's something really serious. Police are everywhere."

Marian clicked onto the news. Shock ran through her at the lead headline: "Two dead at Virginia Tech. Gunman still on the loose." *Only two*, she tried to reassure herself. Couldn't be Caitlin. But there was still no message. Deep inside Marian, like a mother, knew something was wrong. She reached to shut off her computer and saw that the headline had changed. The number of dead had now climbed into the twenties. She raced for her car and called Chris. "Get ready to leave," she said. "We're going down to Virginia."

The weather was still bad. They hit snow going through the mountains. Traffic slowed, then came to a halt. While Chris gripped the wheel, Marian called every hospital and police station within a hundred miles of Virginia Tech. No one could tell her anything. On the radio the news grew grimmer. The death toll rose. The names of the first two victims were released. At least thirty more names would follow. All the while Marian checked her cell phone for the one message she was desperate to get. No "OK." No "O." Nothing.

They finally pulled up at Virginia Tech. Police ushered them through the crowds to a room at the rear of the inn where other families were gathered. A police office and a minister walked up to them. "Part of me wanted to run," Marian wrote, "to run so fast I could get back to yesterday when the only worry I had was a flooded house. Instead, I stood stock-still, bracing for the shock."

"Mr. and Mrs. Hammaren," the officer said, "I'm sorry. Your daughter was pronounced dead at five minutes after ten this morning."

Caitlin's sorority sisters helped them get through the week. In a haze, forcing themselves to move forward, they spoke to the police, cleaned out Caitlin's room and attended a service with more than six hundred other people. Just before they headed back to New York, Marian was given Caitlin's laptop. She looked at it with grief. No more funny e-mails sent from it, or photos with Caitlin's sorority sisters.

Then Marian opened the laptop and saw a small strip of paper taped above the screen. "God," it said, "I know that today nothing can happen that you and I can't handle together."

At home every time Marian picked up her cell phone she expected to hear her daughter's voice. She couldn't go into Caitlin's bedroom. Could barely go upstairs at all. She could talk to Chris but he was suffering just like she was. She needed to talk to someone. The only person she really wanted to talk to was Caitlin. With nowhere else to turn, she started talking to God.

"Why?" she asked again and again. She screamed. She yelled. "How could something like this happen? Why did you let my daughter get taken away from me?"

She picked up books on spirituality at her bookstore and burned through them. She read the Bible. She was looking for something, a response, an answer. In the middle of a book, those earnest words taped to Caitlin's computer would pop into her head, "God, today nothing can happen that you and I can't handle together." What did that mean?

One August day four months after Caitlin's death, Marian was sitting in her backyard, reading. It was a gorgeous summer morning, with the sun pouring down and the breeze shifting the branches of the trees. Not unlike that morning when she and Chris had first loaded up the car and driven Caitlin down to Blacksburg.

Out of the blue, that prayer of Caitlin's sounded in Marian's head: "Nothing can happen that you and I can't handle together." This time the words were being said to Marian. They penetrated her. Deep in her bones she believed them too. She knew with utter conviction that she would see her daughter again. "Lord," she prayed, "I don't understand Caitlin's death. I'm pretty sure I never will. But I know that you're here with me. Because I know you—because you're present in my life—I know that Caitlin is here with me too." She felt God present with her in her misery, God echoing her sorrow.

I once worked on a story with a minister, of all people, who stopped talking to God when his son was born with severe birth defects. The man was in too much of a rage. "After all I've done," he told himself. "After giving myself to others, to God's service, he would do this to me. How dare he!" He preached, he read the Bible to his congregation, said prayers with them, he visited the sick and elderly, but he refused to address God directly. Not a word. He was fed up with God, unspeakably angry.

After a year of this holy silent treatment, he had a disagreement with a friend. They patched it up quickly—it had all been a simple misunderstanding. "I'm so glad you told me you were angry," the friend said. "I needed to know." *I needed to know.*

The parallel in the minister's own spiritual life pierced him with immediate understanding. If he was angry with God, didn't he need to say it? The least he could do was speak out.

He got down on his knees and prayed, all his pent-up anger spewing forth. He told God what he thought, the angry "No's" finally coming out, the recriminations, the hatred, the wounded pride. He couldn't begin to ask for help and he probably couldn't have been helped until they'd had it out.

To not tell God how angry you are is to risk not telling yourself, to keep your feelings bottled up. Marian had every reason to be in a rage. It seems miraculous to me that she understood enough to yell and scream at God, praying "Noooooooooo!" when the news went from bad to worse to devastating. Only then, only when she kept the connection going, refusing to hide her anguish, was there a hint of healing. I don't doubt that she has to relive that prayer of "No" every time April 16 comes around. The pain will always be there, even in the midst of comfort. A friend who lost his daughter twenty-one years ago to a horrific accident says that every anniversary is different, but every anniversary needs to be observed. Sometimes you need to remember the bad times with God to get to the good.

◆ ◆ ◆

Negative emotions get in the way of prayer, especially if they go unacknowledged. "I don't feel like praying," we say. "I'm too angry with God." For me fear is the biggest culprit. I have no desire to pray when fear is driving peace and love right out of my heart. I don't know how to find God when I'm trembling inside and the inner voices block all hope. Where is he? Will I even know him when I see him? On the day of the Resurrection, two of the disciples were headed to a village called Emmaus. They were talking about what had happened when Jesus approached them. They didn't even recognize him.

"What are you discussing with each other?" he asked.

This was when one of them, Cleopas, the only one named in the Gospel, said, "Are you the only stranger in Jerusalem who does not know the things that have taken place there in these days?" (Luke 24: 18). He was incredulous and maybe a bit arrogant, blinded by grief. How could this stranger not know?

"What things?" Jesus asked innocently enough.

Cleopas gave him the full rundown. That Jesus was condemned to death and crucified. That they had hoped he would be the one to redeem their people. That nothing like that had happened. The only disturbing thing was that very morning some women of their group had found Jesus' tomb empty and a vision of angels appeared, saying he was alive. What a frightening story to hear, impossible to comprehend.

"Oh, how foolish you are and how slow of heart to believe," Jesus said. He went on to explain how Scripture had been fulfilled.

Near the village Jesus seemed prepared to leave them, but in keeping with the ancient rules of hospitality, they urged him to come with them. "Stay with us, because it is almost evening and the day is now nearly over."

When he was at the table with them, he took bread, blessed it and broke it and gave it to them. Their eyes were finally opened, they recognized him and then he vanished from sight. Only then could they acknowledge how they'd felt when he first appeared. Only then could they see. "Were not our hearts burning within us while he was talking to us on the road?"

I can hear the cynic say, "If he really was Jesus, why didn't they figure it out? They had enough time with him, after all." I can also think of times when fear and sorrow prevented me from seeing a truth blazing before my eyes. Praying "*Noooooooo!*" is a way to push back at the fear, send it packing.

I've already mentioned how our son Timothy, at age four, broke his femur. It was one of those times when everything seemed to be going wrong.

Of all days, it was Maundy Thursday. I came back to the office from a dentist appointment. One of our assistants looked gravely at me. "Call your wife," she said. I got back to my desk and found several messages from Carol. With each one she sounded a bit more frazzled. The first: "Tim's been in an accident at nursery school. It sounds like he broke something. I'll let you know." Then another message: "We're heading to the doctor's office. It looks bad." Then a third: "The doctor sent us to the X-ray lab at 59th Street. Can you meet us there?"

Obviously this was before the days of cell phones.

I dashed out the door, leaving a quick message at church. "I don't think I'll be able to sing at the service tonight," I told our choir director. "Timothy broke his leg."

The X-ray lab was in a dreary building near St. Luke's–Roosevelt Hospital. I went to the lab on the sixth floor. Then I was sent to the pediatric lab on the tenth floor. Carol and Timo weren't there. "But were they here?" I asked. There was no record, said the receptionist. I called the doctor's office and didn't get a response. I called work to see if Carol had called there—all of these calls made from a corner pay phone. Finally I played back a message on my voice mail from Carol: "Hi, it's me. We're at the Hospital for Joint Diseases down on East 17th."

I considered taking a cab, but now it was rush hour and the subway would be faster. The A train to the L train. At the hospital I asked for Pediatrics. Someone sent me up to the thirteenth floor. I stepped out of the elevator and into the conversation of two doctors.

"It's the worst break I've ever seen on a kid," one said to the other, shaking his head. "Right through his femur. He got hit by a tricycle."

Were they talking about my son? The worst break he'd ever seen on a kid?

"Could you tell me where the pediatric X-ray lab is?" I asked politely.

"You've got to go back downstairs. It's on the third floor."

Finally I found Timothy and Carol, Timo looking small and shocked. He was actually shaking. Carol explained: He'd been in an accident at nursery school. Some kid ran into him with a tricycle.

"That's what some doctor upstairs was saying. The worst break he'd ever seen." The fear started cranking up. ("This is the reason hospital staff is asked never to discuss a case outside of an office or some private space," a friend who works in a hospital told me.)

According to the X-rays the break was in the femur, a big bone to heal. Carol, trying to be brave, with both of us trying not to be alarmist in front of Timo, said, "The doctors say he has to be in traction for twenty-seven days."

In traction?

"He can be at home, can't he?"

"He has to be in traction here at the hospital."

A four-year-old in traction in a hospital bed for twenty-seven days? That sounded like being stuck on a plane for twenty-seven days with a toddler, trying desperately to entertain him and distract him. It was frightening. Unthinkable. How would we handle it?

I spent that first night with Timothy. He was on his back, his leg in a contraption in the air, the sides of his crib like bars on a jail cell. The parents of the kid in the next bed were watching a shoot-'em-up cop movie on TV to distract them from their crying child. At midnight the show was still going on. The loud soundtrack made it impossible to pray. I wouldn't have known what to say anyway.

"Daddy, we're stuck," Timo said, grabbing the bars.

"You'll be okay, honey," I said, struggling to believe it. All I could do was echo his thought: We're stuck. We're stuck. We're stuck. When he finally dozed off, I tried to sleep in the hospital chair. And I tried to pray. Fear was making it impossible. Jesus could have been standing right there in a hospital gown—probably was. I couldn't see him. The only word I could pray was "Noooooooooo!"

◆ ◆ ◆

What comes to the rescue when you're saying no? How do you get out of it? Maybe it's by just saying no that you open yourself up for help. It leads back to that spiritual relinquishment that Catherine Marshall talks about. Say no loud enough and someone will hear. I've already mentioned how Mom and Dad both came out to help us through that rough patch. Our good friends did too. One neighbor actually coordinated a crew to cover our needs. Every night we got the call: "Need anybody to watch the kids? Anybody to do an errand?"

How did Diane and Mike get through his two months in the burn unit? How did my sister manage to take care of her girls, visit the hospital and remain positive through that long ordeal? You can't stay in a high-adrenaline emergency zone forever. You finally collapse. Family and friends came to their rescue too. Their refrigerator was so full of dropped-off meals that I don't think Diane went grocery shopping for two months. People came out of the woodwork. Our prayers, their prayers, became ones of hope and comfort instead of those monstrous prayers of fear. No one would ever ask for any such disasters to come into their lives, and yet, when you live through one, when you get to the other side, even if all you can pray is "No, God, no," you find your faith changed.

Patrick and Carter were fraternity brothers at Birmingham Southern College in Alabama, Patrick a premed. At the end of August, before classes started, they decided to go camping with some other frat brothers in the Sipsey Wilderness, a remote part of north-central Alabama, about seventy miles northwest of Birmingham.

They drove up on a Saturday morning, parked at the end of a rutted dirt road, grabbed their backpacks and tents and made their way up sandstone bluffs into a dense forest. Far from civilization, so far there was no cell phone signal, they set up camp on a rock ledge overlooking a fork of the Black Warrior River. There was a sheer sixty-foot drop to the cold waters below.

After hiking down to the river and swinging like Tarzan from a tree that hung over the waters, they hiked back up to start a fire, put up their tents and build their campsite. They gathered wood, cooked burgers and hot dogs, sang songs around the fire as it got dark. The fire was burning down. "Carter," Patrick said, "could you grab some more wood?" Carter was a sophomore, a year younger than Patrick.

Carter went to their woodpile, picked up a branch that needed to be broken to fit on the fire. He hauled it off to jump on it. No one was paying much attention, but somehow while jumping on the branch, Carter lost his balance and fell. One of the guys turned around and noticed. "Guys, Carter fell off the cliff!"

"Oh, my God, oh, my God, no!" Patrick thought. For a second he couldn't move, couldn't pray, couldn't do anything. Then he cried out, "God, don't let Carter die!"

Maybe it was his premed training or maybe it was the motivation that came with prayer, but Patrick went into action. "Call 911," he told the guys. Then remembered. No cell service for miles. "Forget that. Drive into town and get help!"

Patrick scrambled down the hill. First he looked for Carter on a rocky promontory just thirty feet below the campsite. Nope. He must have fallen all the way into the river. How could he have survived? Patrick raced back to the campsite, got a lantern and a flashlight, and ran down to the water with some of the other guys.

It was pitch dark. He held up the lantern, and could see nothing. At least five minutes must have gone by. Patrick knew from his pre-med classes that if Carter were underwater without oxygen for eight minutes or longer, he'd be brain dead.

*Jump in,* a voice urged Patrick. The voice was quiet and insistent. He dropped the lantern, clamped the flashlight between his teeth and dove in. He stayed down for thirty seconds. Couldn't find him. Swam to a second spot and dove again. Nothing. One more time and his foot hit something. Carter. Patrick grabbed his friend under his arms and dragged him to the surface, then swam him to shore. It was like pulling a dead weight, Carter's mouth wide open, his eyes vacant.

Their buddies were ready to reach for Carter, but again something urged Patrick, *Don't pull him out of the water.* "Just keep his head above water. Hold his neck and stabilize him." He didn't want to risk spinal cord damage.

He listened for a heartbeat. Nothing. Then began mouth-to-mouth resuscitation and chest compressions. He kept trying and trying. Patrick figured his friend had been oxygen-deprived for twelve minutes. No way would he survive. Then came a slight gurgling noise.

Probably the last bit of air escaping Carter's body. But the gurgling came again. And again. Very weak. Was that a heartbeat?

The rescue crew finally arrived. In a matter of minutes they had Carter in a harness and in a medevac helicopter. Patrick and his buddies followed. Patrick didn't say what was on his mind, that if Carter somehow survived, he wouldn't be Carter anymore. He couldn't possibly be. He'd been without oxygen for too long. "No, God, no," came that prayer. *Noooooooooo!*

The only encouraging word from the ER doctor was that they'd done the right thing by keeping him in the river. "The cold water lowered his core temperature and kept him alive. Good thing you knew how to do that."

Patrick couldn't take credit for it. Something—or was it someone?—had told him what to do.

For two weeks Carter was kept in a medically induced coma. Brain scans showed he'd been without oxygen for at least ten minutes. Doctors told his parents to expect the worst. But his family didn't give up hope. Patrick tried not to. Finally the doctors brought Carter out of the coma. "He was the same Carter," Patrick marveled. No permanent brain damage. "Miracle Kid," they started calling him. All those "No's" had turned, amazingly, astoundingly, into a Yes.

Patrick had never been as scared as he was when his friend fell off a cliff into the water, but he never lost touch with God. He acted and his friend survived.

◆ ◆ ◆

A time of mass fear came for the nation on 9/11. Most of us can recall the moment when we looked at TV and said, "No, God." I wasn't in New York that day, but I remember being so frightened after what I saw that I walked outside in the sunshine, just to get away from the brutal images of flames, smoke and massive skyscrapers disappearing in billows of dust. "No, God, no, this can't be happening."

The next day in midtown Manhattan, a familiar view was gone from our south-facing windows at the office. Two enormous buildings that had dominated the skyline were conspicuously missing. We were stunned, numb, angry. Soon all over town eight-by-eleven Xeroxed posters of the missing appeared on lampposts and phone booths, husbands, wives, daughters, sons pictured in happier days. "Have you seen?" "Any information on…" The wanted were the lost. Twenty-four hours after the disaster, police sirens wailed, jangling our nerves. But as the stories were coming in of the people who were gone, there were still stories coming in of the people who were saved. We held on tight to every one of them.

Can I say there's something saintly about Brian Clark and Stanley Praimnath? They wouldn't say that about themselves, but ten years after, they still exude the faith they both say helped them that terrible day. For the tenth anniversary of 9/11 they came into the office for a photo shoot. Stanley brought the business shoes he had worn walking down some eighty stories of the World Trade Center. They still smelled of smoke.

I have met other people who have survived appalling tragedies and still seem haunted by them, the nightmare never ending. Or they haven't wanted to talk about what happened. These two, Brian in particular, have made a point of sharing their story.

They were strangers at the time. Stanley was an assistant vice president in loans operations at Fuji Bank on the eighty-first floor of the South Tower, while Brian worked for Euro Brokers on the eighty-fourth floor. Ever since the first terrorist attack on the World Trade Center back in 1993 Brian had volunteered to be a civilian fire marshal. When the North Tower was hit at 8:46 that morning, he grabbed his flashlight and ordered everyone in the office to evacuate the building. "People are jumping!" someone said from the window. He couldn't bear to look.

Stanley had actually taken the elevator down to the lobby after the North Tower was hit. "The safest place to be is back in your offices," he was told, and he returned to his desk. The offices were still eerily empty when he glanced out the window and saw the plane coming up from the southern tip of Manhattan, traveling unbelievably close to the ground. He watched in horror as it got closer and closer. He could actually see the lettering on the sides. Its nose seemed pointed right at him. He dove under his desk. No, it couldn't be happening. *I'm in your hands, Lord.*

It took him a few moments after the plane hit to stop shaking. His legs felt like jelly. He crawled out from under the desk. The walls in the office had been knocked flat. Papers drifted everywhere. He was chest-deep in plaster and broken furniture. Through the ripped ceiling he could see the floor above.

Brian was escorting a colleague to the ladies' room, flashlight in hand, when the plane hit. The lights went out. Ceiling tiles and air-conditioning ducts broke loose and clattered to the floor. Dust was everywhere. The floor beneath him lurched up. His fire marshal training kicked into gear and he led a group through the darkness toward the stairwell. On the eighty-first floor he ran into two people coming up. "We've just come off a floor in flames," one of them said. "We have to get above them."

Up or down? What was the best thing to do? Both could be deadly.

Just then Brian heard a sound, a muffled voice coming through the stairwell wall: "Help me, somebody. Please help! I can't breathe."

Brian followed the voice. The air was worse than on the stairs, and there was another sharper smell, what he later realized was jet fuel. He wondered if he should turn back. Again came the cry: "Help me!"

"Hang on," he called. He shined his flashlight around. All he saw was a massive wall. Then at the very bottom something moved for a second, caught in the beam of light. A hand. "I see you," he cried.

Stanley was overwhelmed. He wanted to say a thousand prayers right then and there. He couldn't keep his faith to himself. "I have to ask you," he said. "Do you know Jesus?"

"Yes," said Brian, "I go to church every Sunday." Neither of them thought it was an odd conversation to be having at the time.

Stanley pounded on the wall. Brian did too. Piece by piece, they widened the hole. Finally Brian reached in and grabbed Stanley and pulled him through the opening. "My name's Brian," he said.

"I'm Stanley, and you're my brother for life."

The air was getting thicker. "Let's get you out of here," Brian said. They started down the eighty-one flights of stairs. The first flight was almost blocked by wreckage. Stanley hesitated. "Come on," Brian said. "We can do this." He led the way, sliding down a pile of debris.

The sprinklers were running. At about the seventy-ninth floor they saw long cracks in the wall and flames. The heat was terrible, but it was too late to turn back. By the seventy-fourth floor, the air started to clear. They went down, flight by flight, seeing no one. At 9:55, they staggered out onto the concourse. The place was empty. "Go through those doors and run!" a rescue worker told them.

They sprinted across Liberty Street past a maze of trucks, police vehicles and dazed survivors. They didn't stop until they came to Trinity Church. "This man saved my life," Stanley said to a minister standing outside. "He's my guardian angel." They wanted to go inside to thank God and pray for those who were still trapped. For the first time they could look back and see the Trade Center. Brian was struck with horror at the thought of his coworkers who had gone up instead of down. How had they survived? There was a rumbling sound and the top of the South Tower disappeared from sight. Dust filled the air.

They ran for their lives again. At one point Stanley pulled out his business card and put it in Brian's hand. Then they slowed to a walk. Arms around each other, they joined the thousands of others moving toward the East River and the bridges leading out of Manhattan, leading to safety.

Just before they reached the river, Brian and Stanley got separated. For a moment Brian wondered if it was really true. Did Stanley really exist? He reached into his pocket and pulled out the business card.

Later people would say to Brian, "You saved Stanley's life." But as Brian saw it, Stanley saved *his* life. If he hadn't rescued Stanley, what would have been his fate? Ready to give his life to save a stranger, he ended up being saved himself.

Stanley is still a banker but he's also a minister. He often thinks of what Joseph said to his brothers: "You meant evil against me but God meant it for good" (Genesis 50:20). The soles of the shoes he wore that day are melted and caked in ash. He's kept them in a shoebox with the word "deliverance" written on it. "They're kind of like my ark, a reminder of God's presence and the life I owe him," he says.

I was just one of millions who prayed in horror when I watched the disaster unfold on 9/11. None of our prayers reversed the tragedy. The evil had happened. We couldn't rewind the clock or send those fuel-laden jets back. But there is truth in the mystery Stanley Praimnath observed. *You meant evil against me but God meant it for good.* Prayer is a means for extracting the good out of what can only seem bad. At times of crisis anger, fear and shock hit you hard. You don't think you can even move forward. You're trapped, numbed. You cry out to God, "Nooooooooo!" It seems a futile outburst, but that's all you could possibly say. And it's the prayer that keeps you connected. It's the way of reclaiming the good. Both men in Tower Two prayed to God for help. And then they found each other.

## CHAPTER SEVEN

# Sing Your Prayer

*"Alleluia."*

In fifth grade, I was finally old enough to sing in the kids' choir at church. We ran over from school, raced across the flagstones in the church courtyard, kicking up petals from the Iceland poppies. The choir mothers fed us doughnuts, Lorna Doones, Fig Newtons, Dolly Madison cupcakes or whatever they figured would keep us subdued for an hour-long rehearsal. We dashed up the linoleum stairs and took our assigned seats, the boys filling one row—at least I wasn't the only one. The choir director pounded out chords on the piano, then poked at the air, gesturing at our notes in space. We opened our mouths. "God is in this place," we sang. "*Ah-lay-lu-ee-ya.*"

I've sung in big, trained church choirs that appeared on national TV and little ones that barely fielded a voice per part. I was part of the tenor section of the cathedral choir in Florence, Italy, when I sang the "Hallelujah Chorus" one Easter Sunday, failing to make the slightest dent in the way my Italian cohorts pronounced the English words:

"Hay shall r-r-reign for aye-ver and aye-ver." I've happily bellowed out rough-hewn Appalachian tunes in our church choir, pounding my feet against the floor. I love spirituals and gospel and singing praise music with a rock band, rhythmically challenged though I am, but truth to tell, I'm happiest with the old standbys, from "Rock of Ages" to "Amazing Grace."

I would feel robbed if I didn't get to sing in church. With age I can't sustain a long phrase like I used to, and I fear I'm developing a wobble. At some point our choir director is going to tell me, "Rick, you've got a vibrato you could drive a truck through," but with my dying breath, I will sing.

"Dad, don't sing here," my kids exclaim when the spirit moves and I break out in song on the streets of New York or on the subway. Not long ago I was on a subway train heading to work and I heard a West Indian woman singing, "Holy, holy, holy, Lord God Almighty!"

She was coming down the car, passing out Bible tracts. "That's not the tune I know," I told her. "How does that go again?"

"Holy, holy, holy," she sang again and I joined in (I'm a better follower than sight reader). "Which wert, and art, and evermore shall be," we sang together.

The doors opened. "I've got to go. That's my stop," I said, stopping the singing.

"Amen, brother," she told me.

"Amen, sister," I said right back and exited the train.

The Bible is full of singing. The Psalms were all written to be sung, with "lute and harp," "tambourine and dance," "strings and pipe" and "loud clashing cymbals." St. Francis of Assisi and his sworn-to-poverty brothers sang psalms as they wandered the Umbrian hills, preaching to the birds and begging. Paul and Silas sang in jail with their feet in stocks. In a preliterate, preprint era, putting a text to music was a way of remembering it. When you couldn't carry a pocket Bible or have a Bible app on your cell phone you could carry the words in your head, surely the best place for them anyway.

The early church created hymns that clarified their beliefs. Paul is probably quoting one of those early Christian hymns in his epistle to the Philippians (2:10–11): "That at the name of Jesus every knee should bow, of things in heaven and things in earth and things under the earth. And that every tongue should confess that Jesus Christ is Lord." Every tongue confessing like every tongue bursting out in song. In Ephesians 5:14, he quotes another hymn: "Sleeper, awake! Rise from the dead, and Christ will shine on you." Makes me think of a four-part Bach chorale we sing at Advent, "Sleepers, Wake," which is more specifically a reference to the parable of the virgins waiting for the bridegroom with their lit lamps.

I'm terrible at memorizing Bible verses, but certain passages stick with me because I've sung them or heard them sung. "Many waters cannot quench love, neither can the floods drown it" (Song of Solomon 8:7). "O clap your hands, all ye people, shout unto God with a voice of triumph" (Psalm 47:1). "I am the bread of life and he that believe in me shall not slumber" (Job 6:34). When someone reads this passage from Job (19:25) at a funeral—"I know that my Redeemer liveth and that he shall stand on the latter day upon the earth"—how can you not hear it as Handel set it to music in the

*Messiah?* Or for that matter, how can you hear the word *Hallelujah* without singing it? It's alleluia with an "H," impossible for my Florentine choir friends to do.

"But I *can't* sing," I can hear you protesting. "I can't carry a tune in a bucket. Ever since I was in second grade and our music teacher told me to just mouth the words, I've been afraid to sing."

Maybe you can't sing. (How I wish I could give those bad-news music teachers of yore a piece of my mind.) But you can learn. I have a friend who says she can train anyone, even the most tone-deaf, to sing a respectable "Happy Birthday." More importantly, I'd rather stand next to someone singing the wrong notes than think they are too intimidated to sing at all. We'll call it harmony.

My dad always sat in the front pew at church and sang at the top of his voice. The tone was great, the pitch varied. He had about four notes that he could carry—sometimes they were the right notes. What did it matter? My dear colleague Edward Grinnan claims he's the family lip-syncher, the guy who moves his mouth but makes no sound. His tone-challenged mom was more like my dad; she sang at top volume. "God loves my voice," she declared.

"Make a joyful noise to the Lord" says the psalmist (100:1, RSV). Nothing there about making a perfect sound.

Even if you insist on lip-synching, you can still use music to pray. Put the ear buds in, crank up the volume and be that singer of your dreams. Long ago in that upstairs choir room of my childhood, I used to stare at a sign that said in ecclesiastical Gothic script, "He who sings prays twice." I didn't have a clue as to what it meant then. Still not sure I do, except that I know music is a great amplifier of the spirit. It can connect you to the emotional heart of something when you're spiritually numb. I'm sure you've had the experience of listening to some song and being transported right out of a self-pitying, preoccupied state. When you can't find words to help you pray, reach for a song.

Dad's last five months of life were spent in a nursing facility. The wheelchair-bound residents gathered every day in a bright community room for meals and activities, coaxed by a remarkably good-natured staff. They played bingo, watched *Singing in the Rain* on a wide-screen TV and heard Sunday morning church services.

We didn't fool ourselves by saying, "Dad will be coming home soon." This was it, his last spot on earth, a shared room at the end of the hall near a plaque that read, "I was sick and you visited me (Matthew 25:36)." He'd be there till the end. For the rest of the family it was within an hour's drive. For me it was a five-and-a-half-hour cross-country flight. I made the trip once a month, which never felt like enough. When I was back in New York I was always thinking of where Dad lived.

"You should sing for them," Mom suggested.

"Who?"

"Daddy and the others in the community room. They would like that."

"Okay," I said, trusting Mom's instincts.

I printed out words from my big yellow Rodgers & Hammerstein songbook: "Oklahoma!" "Some Enchanted Evening," "Edelweiss,"

"Hello Young Lovers." These were tunes he loved to hear me play on the piano when I was young. It would be a trip down memory lane. But also in those heartbreaking days, practicing the songs was a way of staying in touch. Walking down 34th Street in a cold rain singing to myself the tango of "No Other Love" linked me to a family drama on the sun-drenched West Coast. There is some intriguing research about how loved ones can share the same thoughts though separated by hundreds of miles. We've often run stories of people who had urges to pray for a loved one only to later discover that was just the moment of danger or need. Could Dad sense me singing songs for him far away? I don't know. But I could keep him close through the music.

"Your dad must love to have you sing," friends would say.

"I'd go nuts if I weren't doing it," I would say. It was too hard to process this leave-taking with only monthly cross-country flights.

At the care facility, many of the patients had slipped into dementia. One woman spoke to me only in Korean as though I could understand every word. Another showed off her doll, assuring us that this was her baby. One man always asked me where I'd gone to high school. One woman rocked back and forth in her wheelchair, moaning, "No, no, no, no."

"We have a real treat today," said the activities director when they gathered in the community room. "Mr. Hamlin's son Rick will sing for us."

No piano, no guitar, no music in front of me. I looked at everyone and launched into "The Surrey With the Fringe on Top," hoping I could remember what I'd memorized on Manhattan's cold streets.

Scanning the faces of my audience, I wondered if they were following. What was going on in their minds? Did they recognize the song at all? Halfway through, one woman joined me from her wheelchair. She didn't miss a word, even the tricky part about the "isinglass curtains you can roll right down." Wouldn't you know it, it was the woman whose only word until then had been "No, no, no, no."

I thought I was there for Dad. Maybe I was there for her. She kept on singing from *Oklahoma* and *South Pacific* after my mini-recital was done. She finally went back to her refrain of "No, no, no, no" but at least it had a tune beneath it now, a cheerier one that spoke of a surrey with fringe on top. He who sings prays twice? My prayer had been for some peace of mind. Amplified by the music, it was as though it spread to her.

◆ ◆ ◆

Music cuts right through to our emotional and spiritual needs. It can say what we can't. Not long ago I was working on a *Guideposts* story with *Good Morning America* anchor Robin Roberts. She wrote about her mother, Lucimarian, one of those extraordinarily lucky people who can sit down at a piano and play any tune. From a young age Lucimarian took refuge in singing hymns and accompanying herself at the keyboard. She married Larry Roberts, a career officer in the Air Force and one of the famous Tuskegee Airmen who integrated the military during World War II. After the war, in the early days of their marriage, they were stationed in Japan.

Lucimarian was living with a toddler in a few rooms of a Quonset hut far away from home. "Nothing prepared me for the isolation I felt as the only black woman on a base in a foreign country," she wrote in her memoir, *My Story, My Song*. "On days when the loneliness became almost unbearable, I would go to the base chapel, which was open twenty-four hours a day. I'd slip inside the empty chapel, go straight to the piano and begin to play hymns and sing. By the time I left an hour or so later, I felt revived. I have often wondered what I would have done without the hymns and scripture to comfort me then and countless other times."

Many years later, after a long happy marriage, Larry died of a sudden heart attack. Lucimarian was bereft. She lived in Pass Christian, Mississippi, where they had retired. That first Thanksgiving she went to New York to be with Robin for the holidays. The two were invited to join Robin's colleague Diane Sawyer and Candice Bergen, among others, for Thanksgiving dinner. Robin assured her mom that they didn't have to go. They could do something small, just the two of them, but even in grief, Lucimarian wanted to be with others. She'd always thrived around people.

They went to dinner with Robin's friends (Lucimarian was amused to think that Murphy Brown was passing around the hors d'oeuvres). When they gathered at the table, everyone was asked to make a comment or offer a reflection. *Mom, you don't have to say anything,* Robin thought. Everybody would understand. But when it was Lucimarian's turn, she did what she'd always done.

Her voice soft but still true, she began to sing the old spiritual "We'll Understand It Better By and By." The song contained her sense of loss along with her hope and faith. "By and by, when the morning comes, when the saints of God are gathered home, we'll tell the story how we've overcome..." Soon Diane Sawyer joined in. "For we'll understand it better by and by." How else to take in the unexplainable, how else to get to the other side of grief? When you sing with someone else you share your sorrow. Just two voices in harmony—"wherever two or more are gathered"—is reassurance enough that you're not alone.

Contemporary music has shown us the range of emotion a song can contain. The blues, rap, hip-hop, folk, country, rock can take on remorse, rage, sorrow, pain and praise. The Psalms are prayers with the same outrageous range. What could be more mournful than the opening of Psalm 137? "By the waters of Babylon we sat down and wept." All the misery of a displaced people far from home is in that line. But less often will people quote the end of the same psalm: "Happy shall he be that takes and dashes the little ones against the rocks."

What are we supposed to do with verses like that? They're disquieting, disconcerting. Part of me wants to edit them out of the Bible. What a mistake that would be, like censoring a prayer. I've never heard that vengeful verse set to music but I can imagine singing it with full-throated anger. "God, I'm so angry and lonely and miserable, here's what I wish you would do!" I can also imagine feeling much better after I've sung it. Cleansed, purged, getting something out of my system. We all have enemies. We're supposed to pray about them. Even sing of them. Why should we be surprised when a psalm gets raw? The words that we need to pray or sing can be counterintuitive.

A Jewish friend of mine was talking to me about mourning her mother's death. She decided to observe the religious tradition of saying Kaddish, the Jewish prayer of mourning, for a year. A busy ob-gyn, she managed to go to her synagogue before work every morning and pray with a small gathering. One important part of saying Kaddish is that you are urged to pray with others. In grief you shouldn't be alone.

"What are the words of the prayer?" I asked. "Is it a prayer of lamentation?"

"Not at all," she said, surprising me. "The words are mostly words of praise." On the Internet I found a translation. The key line of the Kaddish prayer is the congregational response: "May his great name be blessed for ever and to all eternity."

Praise. Praise when you've gone through loss. Praise for a year of mourning. Why praise? Because praise is healing. Words of praise said with others take you out of yourself. Praise also puts you back into God's world. Praise, even when it's just said, is a song.

Elizabeth Sherrill has written eloquently of suffering from depression, especially in her early days of marriage, when she was raising young children. She could barely get through a day, frozen in despair. Caring for her children was a daily marathon. John would come home from work and she'd dash upstairs to the attic just to be alone with her sorrow. John would have to listen to her sobs coming through the closed door.

At one point his boss, Grace Oursler, the first editor of *Guideposts* magazine, sat John down and asked him how things were. At first he started by explaining what Tibby was going through. "No," she said, stopping him, "I want to know how *you* are. What is happening with *you*? When someone is sick, everyone in the family suffers. Tell me about you."

John explained how weary he was, how frustrated and angry, how it tore him apart to find his two young boys listening at the door of the room where their mother lay crying, how watching the woman he loved more than anyone in the world suffer was more than he could bear.

"Be praiseful," was her advice.

"Thankful?" he asked.

"No," she corrected, "give praise. Think about the difference between praise and thanksgiving. Thankfulness is us-centered. When things work out the way we want, we're thankful. Praise is God-centered. Praise means becoming aware of God in your life right now. Praise is the beginning of healing."

"Praise him, alleluia" is a phrase we've sung at church, and it circles around in my head. It can be repeatedly endlessly. "All that have life and breath, praise ye the Lord. Sing to the Lord, alleluia." Praise can be the most outrageous, unexpected, wonderful, right thing to do. Think of the hymns we sing. When a minister in our congregation died at a tragically young age, we abided by his wishes and opened the funeral with the most glorious of Easter hymns: "Jesus lives! Thy terrors now can no longer death, appall us. Jesus lives! By this we know, Thou, O grave, canst not enthrall us. Allelluia!"

He demanded that we celebrate a victory, tears in our eyes. The thing is, if you're crying, you can't sing and if you're singing, you can't cry. That day we sang.

◆ ◆ ◆

Singing gives us courage to do what we don't think we can do, from Anna in *The King and I* whistling her happy tune to civil rights activists marching with hymns and spirituals.

Not long ago Leymah Gbowee won the Nobel Peace Prize for helping to bring peace to Liberia. The country was torn by a brutal civil war that had left hundreds of thousands dead, families broken, children maimed, villages abandoned. The women of Liberia were fed up, and through Leymah's leadership they began a series of protests in a field near the fish market of Monrovia, the capital.

"In the past, we were silent," Leymah could say to the crowd. "But after being killed, raped, dehumanized and infected with diseases and watching our children and families destroyed, war has taught us that the future lies in saying no to violence and yes to peace. We will not relent until peace prevails."

The women all wore white, as Leymah wrote in her memoir, *Mighty Be Our Powers.* "Liberian women love to dress up, but we'd come to the field completely bare of makeup and jewelry, in the kind of 'sackcloth and ashes' described in the Book of Esther, where the heroic queen stands up to save her people from extermination."

There was a very real threat of violent reprisals from President Charles Taylor. His security service was notorious for torturing and killing opponents. His control over the country was brutal.

The women sat outside in the fierce heat, a hundred degrees in the sun, holding up signs that proclaimed, "The women of Liberia want peace." They prayed for courage, the Christians turning to the Psalms, the Muslims praising Allah, and all of them sang. In the remarkable documentary about Leymah and the women of Liberia *Pray the Devil Back to Hell*, you can hear them chant and sing. The music of their voices rises from the field, magnifying their power, connecting them with their Creator. Even the slogan "We want peace, no more war" they turned into a song.

Those protests were the beginning of change. Leymah herself is quick to admit her flaws and honest about her need for faith. Like Moses, she seems the unlikeliest choice for a leader, an unwed mom, the survivor of an abusive relationship, a woman who had to struggle to find her own voice. At one point someone warned her father, "Talk to your daughter – she's putting your family at risk."

He shook his head and said firmly, "God sent that girl. You will see something good come of it."

"We are tired of suffering—we want peace," the women chanted, the sound of their voices giving each other courage. "We are tired of running—we want peace." The battle for peace was fought with prayer and song.

In another international trouble spot, Haiti, the poorest country in the Western Hemisphere, hymns seemed to be all that were holding the people together. After the earthquake that devastated Haiti in 2010, rescue workers noted people singing. Alison Thompson was one of them.

Alison became a full-time volunteer almost by accident. A freelance filmmaker, she was living in New York when the World Trade Center was hit. As soon as she heard the news on 9/11, she put on her rollerblades and skated downtown, thinking she might be able to help. After all, in her native Australia, her father was a preacher and her mother ran a hospital. She often volunteered at her mother's hospital but she didn't really have any disaster-relief training.

She was skating against the traffic, people covered with dust and ash looking frightened and dazed, trying to get away. She reached Ground Zero and heard a loud rumble. She darted under a UPS truck. The second tower was collapsing. She said a quick prayer for help, then darted out. How could she help?

There were plenty of first responders and professionals looking for survivors trapped under the debris. They had the right training and skills. But who was going to rescue them when they collapsed under the daunting workload or the hopelessness of the task? No one wanted to leave the area but they were spent. They needed encouragement and rest. She could help them. With a friend, Alison commandeered an abandoned bar, put out a sign that said "Ground Zero First Aid Station" and spent the next few days cleaning faces, giving water, offering hugs to exhausted workers. When she was too tired to do much more she skated home to get some rest, but then skated right back, eventually volunteering with the Red Cross. As she puts it, she skated into a whole new role: professional volunteer.

When a terrible tsunami hit Southeast Asia in 2004, she was watching the news. "I'm going there," she told herself. Once again, she had no idea how she could help, but she emptied her minuscule bank account, borrowed a friend's frequent flier miles and flew to Sri Lanka, staying there for the next fourteen months. In a small, devastated village she helped build a hospital and an open-air soup kitchen. She played with the children and organized other volunteers like herself to bury the dead. She even established a tsunami early-warning system.

She went to New Orleans after Katrina, no longer an inexperienced amateur. Within days of the Haiti earthquake she gathered enough medical supplies and equipment to fill an airplane and flew to Port-au-Prince, the stricken capital.

Her group quickly established an outdoor hospital on a golf course in Haiti. Soon they were treating a thousand people a day. That first night, though, as she was trying to sleep, Alison heard singing wafting through the bushes and trees. Three o'clock in the morning and people were singing. A disaster had devastated their impoverished country and their response was music. Hymns. It sounded like a chorus of angels. Where was it coming from?

She got up from her tent before the dawn and followed the sounds. She found lines of refugees, survivors of the quake, waiting in line for food, their stomachs empty but their spirits full of praise.

In the days that followed, a pastor formed an open-air church near the hospital, and every day, when Alison was exhausted from her work at the hospital, she would go to the spontaneous services, raising her hands and singing with the people. The music became her source of healing, praise an unexpected response to misery. She sang to renew her spirit, praying with song.

"Have an eye to God in every word you sing," wrote John Wesley in his preface to *Sacred Melody*, written in 1761. "Aim at pleasing Him more than yourself or any other creature. In order to do this, attend strictly to the sense of what you sing, and see that your heart is not carried away with the sound, but offered to God continually."

Music is inspired and inspiring. Songs can come straight from the Holy Spirit and can administer the comfort of the Spirit. They can be offerings *to* God, but they can also be offerings *from* God. "Come down, O Love divine/Seek Thou this soul of mine,/ And visit it with Thine own ardor glowing," goes the old hymn, a tune that makes me feel it's doing the work of the words. No wonder we often picture angels singing, God's messengers reaching out to us with music. I once interviewed Noel Paul Stookey, songwriter and singer in the folk trio Peter, Paul and Mary, and he told me about a song that came straight from the Almighty. In this case even the words were God's.

Noel dropped out of college and moved to New York City. He had no career plans. He gravitated to the coffeehouses in Greenwich Village to play chess. One night he noticed a stage being constructed in the corner of a coffeehouse and the manager told him auditions for entertainment would be held later in the week. Relying on nothing more than the songs he had written in high school and college, he was suddenly in show business.

He was put together with Mary Travers and Peter Yarrow and they formed Peter, Paul and Mary. Soon their songs, like "Lemon Tree," "If I Had a Hammer" and "Puff (The Magic Dragon)," were on the radio and on top of the charts. The fame was heady. They were performing 150 nights a year, appearing on TV, making recordings, but Noel felt something was missing. He felt he was losing touch. "Read the Bible," a friend advised. He began at Genesis and read right through. He started praying regularly too, asking God the smallest questions: "Shall I take this elevator?" "Shall I sit here?" "What would you have me say?"

When Peter was getting married he asked Noel if he would bless the wedding by singing at it. "Of course," Noel said. But what would he sing? He would have to ask God.

Home from a tour, Noel retreated to his basement studio. He tuned up his twelve-string guitar and then sat in silence. "Lord," he prayed, "nothing would bless this wedding more than your presence. How would you manifest yourself?"

The lyrics came:

*I am now to be among you at the calling of your hearts,*
*Rest assured this troubadour is acting on My part.*
*The union of your spirits here has caused Me to remain,*
*For whenever two or more of you are gather in My name*
*There am I, there is love . . .*

He put them together in a song. About an hour before the wedding he sang them first to his wife, Betty. "It's beautiful," she said, "but they won't understand 'I am now to be among you.' They're going to think you're presuming to be God."

He took his wife's advice and changed the words at the last minute to "He is now to be among you..." He sang it that way for Peter's wedding and expected that he'd never sing the song again.

But several weeks later at a Peter, Paul and Mary concert Peter asked, "When are you going to sing that song you sang at my wedding?"

"But it was just for you, just for your wedding," Noel explained.

"My bride is out there," Peter said. "Would you sing it for her?"

He sang it that night and for the rest of the tour. The song seemed to have larger appeal than he expected. "Is this what you wanted, Lord?" he asked God. "Did you mean the song for everyone?"

The answer seemed to be yes. But this posed a technical problem for Noel. He wanted to include "The Wedding Song" on an album he was recording but how would he copyright it? The song hadn't come from him.

I remember sitting with Noel over breakfast at a New York diner when we talked about this, my tape recorder running. "Other songs I've written have been inspired by my faith, but this one really did come directly from God," he said. Witness the lyrics. "If I didn't copyright it somehow, the record company would get all the profits and that didn't seem right. But I couldn't rightly copyright it in my name either."

In the end he copyrighted the song to a foundation to oversee the publishing rights. Any money the song earned could be distributed to worthy causes. By now millions of dollars have gone to charitable organizations all over the US. "It belongs to every bride and groom who ever had a good friend strum a guitar and sing at their wedding," Noel says. "God gave me a song. It was mine to give away."

◆ ◆ ◆

The people you sing with become a part of you. After they're gone, you can still hear them. I think the sound of everyone who has ever sung at our church is buried in the walls of the place, and all their "alleluias" come echoing back whenever we sing. They make up that "great cloud of witnesses" the Bible talks about. If you've sung harmony with someone, you especially miss their part when they're gone. When Mary Travers died in 2009, Peter and Noel went back on the road to do a series of farewell concerts, one in each city where they had performed together. On Mary's parts in classics like "Leaving on a Jet Plane," they would encourage the audience to sing her line. The tours weren't meant to go on forever. Just this last good-bye with the two-thirds of the trio that was still left. She was gone but she was still there.

Charley was one of my dearest singing buddies. We met in a small, close-harmony, all-male a cappella group in college at Princeton. He was a baritone, I a first tenor. On a winter's night my freshman year, I was initiated into the group when Charley and some of the other guys burst into my dorm room, startling my roommate as they burst into song: "My comrades when I'm no more drinking, but sick with gout and palsied lie...believe me then the end is nigh." An old song that was the group's rallying cry. Their serenade meant I had passed muster. I was in and this was the proof, a bunch of guys waking me up at 2:00 AM.

We sang "My Comrades" on campus under neo-Gothic arches, our voices bouncing off the old stone walls. We performed it on road trips to Florida and at homecoming concerts. We did it at women's colleges, where we teamed up with all-female a cappella groups. In diminished numbers, Charley and I and another pal crooned it on backpacking tour in England. We sang it at graduation, a reminder of how we'd bonded in our bright college years, and sang it at reunions with wives and kids in tow. Even though the lyrics promised death: "When I die, this day or tomorrow, my testament's already made…" we never thought of death singing it. That was the arrogance of youth. It was just an old drinking song that made us giddy, especially the way the group performed it, breaking our semicircle and shaking each other's hands.

Then we sang it at Charley's funeral.

In his early forties, Charley was diagnosed with ALS, Lou Gehrig's disease. There is no cure. The first sign was an ache and tremor in Charley's hands. He was a college professor, editing countless papers and pounding out comments on his computer. He thought he had carpal tunnel syndrome. It was something much worse. The first time I saw him after the diagnosis he was walking with a limp and using a cane. He had two sets of twins, one year old and three years old, and they were tumbling all over him like puppies. "If this is death," I thought, "it wouldn't be so bad." His super-organized wife, Lynn, had already installed wheelchair ramps in their suburban Boston home. She would be ready.

"So I know this ALS has hit your hands and your legs," I said to him, "but I sure hope it hasn't affected your voice."

"Hambone," he called me by a college nickname, "you haven't changed a bit."

"Can you sing?" I asked, ready to launch into a verse of "My Comrades," at least for the kids' benefit.

He shook his head and spoke in an awkward, unmodulated tone: "My breathing's not so good. It's hard to hold a note."

I visited Charley six months later at his family's place in Maine. By then he couldn't feed himself. He was fine with a straw but needed help with a spoon. We sat on the deck, Charley in a wheelchair. I spooned him his yogurt as I'd done with my kids, and I kept missing his mouth. I started giggling and he did too as it dribbled down his chin.

"Hambone," he said, "you were never good for much."

The next time I saw him he was on a feeding tube with round-the-clock care, mostly physical therapy students on eight-hour shifts. He was in a hospital bed set up in his living room. He had a computer close by to communicate with the outer world, and a TV across the room so he could watch *The Little Mermaid* and *Beauty and the Beast* and *Peter Pan* with his kids. They would race through the room while one of the students and Lynn would lift him up with the help of a harness—it took two of them—so they could change the sheets or he could sit in his wheelchair. Every twenty minutes the aide would use a suction machine to suck out the phlegm in his mouth that could choke him or saliva that he couldn't swallow.

He couldn't speak, couldn't nod, but he could blink and he could smile. He had an alphabet on a small board in three rows and if he wanted to say something, you pointed at each row until he smiled or blinked; then you halted there and went through the letters, "H, I, J, K, L, M, N, O..." until he stopped you.

You couldn't finish a word for him. You had to let him have his full say. I remember asking, innocently enough, "How are you?" We spent fifteen minutes working through the answer: "O-U-T T-O L-U-N-C."

"Out to lunch," I leapt to the conclusion.

But he gestured with his eyes. There was more. We went back to the letters and he spelled out: "A-S A-L-W-A-Y-S." No use finishing his thoughts. With ALS your body gives out but your mind doesn't go and I couldn't deny Charley a chance to complete a self-deprecating thought. He was still Charley.

This was the deal he and Lynn had made. It would have been easier to have him in a nursing home, but he wanted to live as long as possible with his kids around so that they would at least have some memory of him.

For two years Lynn and Charley kept life in the living room going. I went up to Boston a couple of times just to offer another pair of adult hands. Frankly I wasn't much help with Charley but I could read books to the kids and give them their baths and wash the dishes for Lynn. I remember giving their three-year-old son Nick a bath and launching into an old cowboy song, "Out in Arizona where the bad men are, there's nothing there to guide you but the evening star..."

"That's a song your daddy taught me," I said. Charley and I sang it in England as we wandered around the gardens at Blenheim and later when we strolled down the streets around Piccadilly, American boys singing about cowboys and the prairie. "You should hear him do it." Then it dawned on me. Little Nick had never heard his daddy sing. He'd never been to any of the reunions where we lined up for the old repertoire. He'd never known what his dad sounded like on a lullaby. Without that, how well could he know his dad? Was Charley really Charley without song?

I dried Nicky off and went downstairs. "I taught him the tenor part to 'My Comrades,'" I told Charley. "That's all he'll ever need."

Charley gave me his "out-to-lunch-as-always" look.

One summer weekend I drove up from New York and walked into the house—the door was always open. Lynn and the kids had gone to the town pool. "Hey Charley," I said, "it's Hambone." He still had that dazzling smile. The PT student was in the middle of bathing him, an extraordinarily complicated process involving the harness to raise Charley's six-foot-four frame. I sat in a chair and waited. A visiting nurse arrived. With help from the PT student Charley explained how he'd almost choked. For a moment he couldn't breathe. It was very scary. He could have died. You could still see the fear in his eyes.

"Of course you could have died," I thought. "You are dying. That's what's happening. That's what ALS means." And yet he wasn't dying. He was living. Life was raging on around him. He was there for the report cards and piano practicing and Suzuki violin squeaking. He could admire the soccer trophies and the Halloween ballerina and see the ball thrown across his bed or rolled under it. He listened to the stories of Madeline and Eloise and Bambi and Barney.

Charley had almost finished his bio for our college class's twenty-fifth reunion book. One finger could still wiggle enough to register yes or no on the computer as it scrolled through the alphabet, his finger picking out the words in the same way that his mind picked out letters from the alphabet board. In December he had a stroke and slipped into a coma. He died two days later. It was a shock even if it wasn't a surprise. Somehow I expected him to go on for many more years.

I thought the funeral was going to be miserable, Lynn looking brave in the front pew with the two sets of twins, the rest of us weeping uncontrollably. But it was a joyous occasion. Everybody in that church had somehow participated in Charley's long battle with ALS. They'd brought casseroles or babysat the kids or raked the yard or given books and videos or sat by Charley's bed. We'd been part of Charley's life, not death.

We sang something dignified and holy at the service, full of alleluias, but after the service in the church hall, it was "My Comrades" once again. "But die I this day or tomorrow, my testament's already made, my burial from your hands all borrowed but without splendor or parade…" The words rang truer than we could ever grasp when we first learned them. Life was long or short but the important thing was to go out singing with your comrades.

The songs that help me pray are not all religious or spiritual. I don't think God minds. As long as they link me back to him. "God, how can I get through sorrow? How am I going to manage the misery of survivor's guilt?" With every milestone I thought of all the stuff Charley was missing. That is the heartbreak of someone you love dying too young. Charley, you would have had a blast at our reunion; Charley, you should have heard us old grads singing again—boy, we could have used you on the baritone line. Charley, you would have been proud at your kids' graduations and their school plays and their soccer games and concerts and seeing the girls dressed up for the prom. Charley, you missed most of Harry Potter. Charley, buddy, I still hear you sing.

Charley taught me that how we die is not something we do just for ourselves. It is the last thing we do for those who love us. I like to think I'll be as feisty and good-natured and funny as Charley was to the bitter end, but even now, a dozen years after his death, I'm not so sure. As long as I have music to help, music around me to ease the way, singing friends even if I can't sing, a million hymns in my head to help me pray. As long as I have alleluias.

## CHAPTER EIGHT

# A Classic Prayer to Focus Your Thoughts

*"Jesus Christ, have mercy on me, a miserable sinner.
Make haste to help me. Rescue me and save me.
Let thy will be done in my life."*

The Jesus Prayer is a prayer from the Eastern Orthodox tradition going back to the Desert Fathers. "Jesus Christ, have mercy on me, a miserable sinner" is the heart of it.

It's easy to learn and so short you can repeat it in your head without anyone knowing you're praying. I find it a godsend when I'm sitting in a meeting, going cross-eyed trying to follow some boring PowerPoint presentation. Who needs to know I'm praying silently? I've found it useful in church meetings too (just because a meeting happens at church doesn't mean it can't be a trial of Christian charity). "What am I doing?" I ask myself. "Why am I here?" The Jesus Prayer restores my focus.

My first acquaintance with it came in college when I read J. D. Salinger's novella *Franny and Zooey*. It's really two short stories back to back, and in the first Franny Glass is on a date with her boyfriend. They're headed to the Yale game, played at what I like to imagine is my own alma mater, Princeton, and over lunch she is spiraling into a meltdown. What she clings to is a book, *The Way of the Pilgrim*, about a Russian peasant who wanders the countryside repeating to himself the Jesus Prayer: "Jesus Christ, have mercy upon me, a sinner..." He repeats it a thousand times a day, then several thousand, the words calming the spirit. I could picture Franny at one of those restaurants I knew from my college days—probably the Annex, with its red-and-white checkered tablecloths and knotty-pine walls. She's smoking cigarettes, eating nothing, crying in the restroom and muttering to herself a prayer culled from a nineteenth-century Russian text. The perfect combination of self-indulgent torpor and collegiate angst.

Several years later I was looking for help in my prayer life. I wanted to find someone I could check in regularly with, someone who would keep me honest and ask me questions. Someone to whom I could say, "Do you really think God is telling me what I think he's telling me?"

I kept putting off the search. It would be one big bother, I told myself. I didn't have time for one more person in my life. There weren't enough hours in the day to see the friends I had. My colleague Peola Hicks calls this "prayer paralysis." You know you should do something but you don't move. You get stuck. But then if you hold that need long enough you'll meet it.

Sitting on the subway one morning, eyes closed, train rumbling, I said, "I know there's someone out there who can teach me more about prayer, someone I can meet with regularly, someone I can pray with and ask any stupid question I have." I got bolder with my request. "I've got friends my age I already meet with. We unload about all sorts of stuff, about the economy, our jobs, our families. But I'd like someone a little older, more experienced, wiser.

"It shouldn't be someone from work," I went on, "or someone from our church. It should be someone outside of my day-to-day world who will challenge me more and give me a different perspective. And it should be someone who lives in New York City or close enough so it's easy to meet."

The name came to me as clear as day: Arthur Caliandro.

Naturally there was more prayer paralysis. How could I ask Arthur? As the senior pastor at Marble Collegiate Church, he had a congregation of thousands and a TV congregation of thousands more. He was way too busy. He'd followed in Norman Vincent Peale's footsteps and led a dynamic ministry. I'd met him through the magazine and admired him, but this would be a huge imposition.

As soon as I said, "That won't work," the thought came back to me: *Isn't he exactly what you said you wanted, wise and knowledgeable, and not a member of your church? He works only a couple of blocks from your office. It wouldn't be hard to get together.*

I made plenty of excuses, postponing the call. Finally I got fed up with myself for procrastinating. I picked up the phone, left a message with his assistant, and hoped that was that. He called back within an hour. I blurted out: "Arthur, I know this is an outrageous request, but I've been looking for someone to meet with regularly and talk about our prayer lives. Your name keeps coming back to me. You've got a million things on your plate..."

"Let's have lunch next week," he said.

"Really?" I asked. "You have time for this?"

"Of course."

We kept it up for eighteen years.

At that first lunch at a dimly lit place filled with businessmen in dark suits and loud ties, he brought up the Jesus Prayer. "Do you pray regularly?" I asked him.

"First thing in the morning I sit by myself in the den," he said. "I have a long list of people who've asked for prayers, but even before I mention them, I start out with the Jesus Prayer. Are you familiar with it?"

"Maybe," I said. "How does it go?" I reached for more butter for my roll.

"This is the version I use." He gazed from our table in the back corner of the restaurant to the bar and the few windows in the front. "Jesus Christ, have mercy on me. Make haste to help me. Rescue me and save me. Let thy will be done in my life."

He said it again and I repeated it to myself.

"Those aren't the exact words of the traditional prayer," he said. "I've expanded the end because I'm always looking for guidance and I need to be rescued. Am I doing what Jesus has called me to do? Am I following God? Am I doing what he's asked of me? Am I becoming his follower? I say it a lot."

"How often?"

"Dozens of times a day. Whenever I need it. It keeps me focused. You might try it."

Indeed I would. I muttered it to myself as I headed back to the office. I used it on the subway after I said my psalms. I looked for it in my old copy of *Franny and Zooey*. I've turned to it when anxiety and worry threatened to undo me. I've said it in doctors' offices and hospital waiting rooms when worst-case scenarios were all I could think of. And like I said, I've used it in the middle of meetings when I feared I was going to blow a gasket. I even made it the centerpiece of a romance novel I wrote a few years ago (*Reading Between the Lines*, if you must know, and yes, to my amazement, it's still in print).

The prayer has been a welcome companion, a reaffirmation of faith in a few words, a quick reminder of my priorities. Jacob Astley, during the English Civil War, proclaimed famously before the Battle of Edgehill in 1642, "O Lord, thou knowest how busy I must be this day. If I forget thee, do not thou forget me." Then he said, "Boys, march." The Jesus Prayer is that in-the-trenches prayer I say so I *won't* forget him. Its meditative power lies in its distillation of the essentials.

Just from the opening, "Jesus Christ, have mercy on me..." comes the reminder of *whose* we are. You can pledge your life to Jesus, have an on-the-road-to-Damascus experience, but you still need to keep connecting. The Lord's Prayer is the prayer Jesus taught us. The Jesus Prayer is one directed *to* him. As my colleague Lemuel Beckett in the prayer division at Guideposts said to me, "What an honor that we get to pray directly to Jesus. It makes me feel like a king." It's a relationship prayer: This is who I am, Lord, and this is who you are to me. But to remember who Jesus is I need to delve back into the Scriptures, which is a sort of prayer, and I look to how others have followed Jesus.

Richard Stearns is the president of World Vision, the multibillion-dollar humanitarian organization. By any standard he would have been considered a serious Christian long before he took the job. It wasn't always so.

In business school he was a hard-headed atheist. All he wanted to do was get his degree, become the CEO of some Fortune 500 company and get rich. His girlfriend Reneé broke up with him when he told her he'd never follow her in faith. Then he started reading the Bible and other books on religion and philosophy. Gradually he became convinced that Jesus Christ was God's son and one day he fell to the floor and cried out, "My Lord and my God!" He committed himself to following Jesus for the rest of his life.

For twenty-five years the fruits of that decision seemed apparent. He and Reneé got married, had five children, lived in a ten-bedroom farmhouse. He became the CEO of Lenox, one of the world's largest makers of fine china. He had a luxurious office at Lenox headquarters, a cherry-wood desk, oil paintings on the walls, a private bathroom, a Jaguar in the CEO's reserved spot. He and Reneé attended church regularly. They tithed, participated in Bible studies, supported missions. God had blessed them and they gave back.

One day Richard got a call from Bill Bryce, an old friend from church who had moved away to take a job raising money for World Vision. "Hi, Rich," Bill said. There was something funny in his voice.

"Everything okay?" Richard asked.

"Sure," Bill said. "It's just that our president is leaving World Vision." Then came the weird part. "I've been praying, Rich, and the thing is, God told me you're going to be the next president of World Vision. I know it sounds crazy, but I'm certain God spoke to me."

Richard was just as certain that he was totally unqualified for the job. He had no experience leading a charity. He didn't know anything about the challenges of international relief. He had a good job that paid well, one he liked. "No," he said. "I'm not interested." That would be that, he figured. Occasionally he heard a bit more from Bill about how the job search was going but that was it.

Then he got a call from a job recruiter. "Rich, I'm Rob Stevenson, a recruiter for World Vision. They're looking for a new president."

"Did Bill Bryce put you up to this?" Richard asked suspiciously.

"Bill who? No, I got your name from a list of World Vision donors." Did Richard know of any possible candidates for the job?

"You'd have to be part CEO, part Mother Teresa, part Indiana Jones," he said. "I don't know anyone like that."

"What about you? You interested?"

"Me? I run a luxury-goods company. I don't know anything about international relief." Again Richard insisted he wasn't qualified.

The recruiter persisted and then he too said an odd thing. "You're not going to believe this, but while we've been talking I've sensed the Holy Spirit telling me that we ought to meet. I've talked to two hundred people so far and you're the first I've had this feeling about."

Needless to say, Richard was getting very uncomfortable.

Rob asked another question. "Are you willing to be open to God's will for your life?"

Richard wanted to drop the phone. "Of course," he stammered, "but I'm pretty sure this isn't it..."

"Let's find out. Have dinner with me."

The conversations continued. To his chagrin Richard Stearns ended up on the shortlist for the World Vision job. In interview after interview he tried to explain why he was a terrible fit. To no avail. Finally he got a congratulatory phone call: He got the job!

How had this happened? He'd done all he could to discourage the search committee. The position fit no definition of God's plan that he understood. He hadn't gone to business school to run a nonprofit. What about the kids' college tuition bills? Reneé was no help. "You never know what God might have in store," she said. "We need to be open to his leading."

On the day he was to fly out to World Vision headquarters in Seattle and see if this offer was something he wanted to pursue, he got another call and another offer altogether, one far more lucrative. Keith, a successful tableware executive, was buying an English china company and planning to merge it with his own. He wanted Richard to be the CEO of the new merged company. He'd even get a ten percent stake in the business.

Richard explained that he had another offer he needed to check out first, one with a charity. He didn't mention the name of the organization.

"That's admirable," Keith said. Out of the blue Keith launched into a story about a girl he and his wife had sponsored in India through a relief organization. They did it after their own daughter had died. That simple act of helping another child had eased their grief. "The charity that put me in touch with her was absolutely wonderful," he said. "They're called World Vision."

Richard was stunned. By the time Keith finished speaking Richard seemed to hear another voice. He realized that he and Reneé were witnessing something profound, God working directly in their lives, showing them that his plan involved something more amazing than they could have imagined.

"My corporate career, my comfortable life, my safe and tidy church involvement," Richard wrote, "all of it was just prologue, maybe even a distraction from serving the Jesus I had committed my life to twenty-five years earlier. I knew then that if I truly wanted to follow that Jesus, I would have to follow the one who gave himself for the poor and dispossessed."

Following Jesus can take you right out of your comfort zone. Had Richard Stearns missed his calling? Did it take him twenty-five years to understand where Jesus really wanted him to be or were those years meant as preparation for where he was supposed to go? In the end his prayer life led him to do something that he never would have guessed, the exact opposite of following the path of least resistance. "Jesus Christ, have mercy on me, a miserable sinner...Let thy will be done in my life." That's not something you say once and have done with it. You say it over and over, searching for the way, like Richard.

Another Jesus follower whose journey amazed and touched me was Scott Morris, a doctor and ordained minister. Even as a boy in Sunday school, Scott was struck with how often Jesus was healing people, how much he cared about the sick. One Sunday, sitting in the pews of his big Atlanta church, he went through the Gospels and started adding it up. "Do you know that over a third of the gospels are about health?" he told his mother that day at dinner. "And in the book of Acts I found nineteen examples of healing by Christ's followers."

Why didn't they do more at his Methodist church for the sick? They put people on the prayer lists or the pastor would visit them in the hospital. Maybe his mom or some of the ladies would make a casserole. That was it. They helped but they didn't heal like Jesus.

If Scott was going to be like Jesus, he figured he should become a doctor. He was a good student and he assumed he was up to the challenge. But one semester of organic chemistry at the University of Virginia did him in. He was miserable. It wasn't the subject matter, which fascinated him. It was the competitiveness of the other premed students. "They hardly cared about what they were learning," he wrote. "All they wanted was to get top grades."

Scott decided to go to seminary instead. He would become a minister.

Two things happened there. In a seminar on counseling the chronically ill he was assigned a patient named Sidney Tillery at the VA hospital. Scott arrived with a slew of questions. Even though he was headed for the ministry, he was still interested in health. Where did Sidney feel the pain? How bad was it? What was it like, eating, sitting, sleeping? At the end of the interview Sidney asked, "Want to play cribbage?"

"I've never played before," Scott said.

"I'll teach you," Sidney said.

That was the beginning of their friendship. Week after week they played cribbage. Scott gave up his list of questions. He learned how to listen. He saw how a chronic illness did its most crippling damage to the spirit. "Your patients will become your teachers," his professor had said. Sidney Tillery taught him how to reach beyond someone's physical aches and pains to minister to their soul. In essence, Jesus' healing mission came alive to him over the cribbage board.

The second thing that changed Scott's trajectory was a pamphlet he saw in the chaplain's office: "How to Start a Church-Based Clinic." He called the writer, did some research and discovered others who'd started church-based clinics for the poor. A light bulb went off in his head: *This is what I want to do with my life.* This was exactly what he'd been looking for. He'd start a church-based clinic for the poor. They'd use the best that modern medicine had to offer and the spiritual tools Christ gave. He'd be both minister and doctor.

With the seminary's support he went back and took the premed classes he needed, then enrolled in med school. With both an MD and an MDiv, he joined the staff of St. John's United Methodist Church in Memphis as an associate pastor and laid out his vision. In a year they opened the Church Health Center in an old house across the street from the church. There was only one nurse and Scott. They saw twelve patients that first day.

Today, over twenty-five years later, they have a staff of 220 and some 55,000 patients. Scott is a busy man but he's never forgotten the lesson of the cribbage board. He still sees patients one-on-one and listens to them.

Most of them are the poorest of the poor. They have worked hard their whole lives, tough manual labor. Often their families have broken up and they've seen their lot of sorrow—drugs, violence, poverty. But when he asks them how they are, they will say, "I'm blessed."

Some of them bless him quite literally. They lay their hands on him and pray over him. They remind him that he is not the healer. God is, and it is the duty of the church to participate in that work. This was the calling Scott discovered when he was a kid thumbing through a Bible in the pew. Jesus cared about the sick. And Scott has made it his life's work to follow Jesus in that passion.

Perhaps it will sound like a wild exaggeration if I tell you that in praying the Jesus Prayer I feel like I'm taking part in the journey that Richard Stearns and Scott Morris have taken. I don't think my meandering footsteps have come close to the paths they have forged or the extraordinary work they have done, but they are models. Something to bump up against and stretch myself around. I look to see if God's moving in my life like he moved in theirs.

"Jesus Christ, have mercy on me, a miserable sinner," I pray in the middle of a very busy life. "Make haste to help me. Rescue me and save me. Let thy will be done in my life." There are a thousand and one distractions to put me off track. The worst is when I congratulate myself, as Richard Stearns used to, and say, "I go to church regularly. I give generously. I sing in the choir. I read the Bible. I'm doing okay, right?" Not with a self-righteous, pharisaical attitude like that.

Not long ago I edited a story by Bear Grylls. Before I worked with him I knew nothing about his faith. I just knew him as the British adventurer on the TV show *Man vs. Wild* who ventured into some of the most dangerous places on earth—remote jungles, stinking swamps, forbidding mountain ranges, searing deserts. He was always seen getting out of tight spots, dodging a huge croc, avoiding a vicious snake, surviving whitewater rapids and describing what was happening in his bloke-next-door accent. But then I learned about an off-camera turnaround from his boyhood.

Like others in his distinguished military family he went off to boarding school at a young age. As a boy, faith had come very naturally to him. Life was full of outdoor adventures that his father devised and Bear relished, like climbing up a sheer cliff and pretending that they were lobbing grenades at the enemy. God seemed present in every challenge and he talked easily and openly to Jesus. But in school he was forced to sit through long chapel services with prayers in Latin and people droning on. "I thought that I had got the whole faith deal wrong," he wrote. "Maybe God wasn't intimate and personal but was tedious, judgmental, boring and irrelevant." The instinctive faith he had known evaporated.

Then he learned that his godfather Stephen had died. Stephen had been his father's best friend and was like a second father to Bear. "He came on all our family holidays and spent almost every weekend with us in the summer, sailing with Dad and me," Bear wrote. "He died very suddenly of a heart attack."

The day he got word of his godfather's death, he went out to the school grounds and climbed a tree. Sitting there in the branches he prayed the simplest, most heartfelt prayer of his life. "God, if you're like you were when I used to know you, will you be that again? Comfort me."

"Blow me down if he didn't do just that!" Bear Grylls told me in that inimitable British accent.

"It is a sign of great strength to need Jesus," he wrote in his story. "My faith is about being held, comforted, forgiven, strengthened and loved. Faith in Christ has been the great empowering presence in my life."

Strength comes from showing your need, exposing your vulnerabilities, especially in prayer. The people Jesus helped in his ministry were the ones who approached him in absolute humility—Nicodemus coming to him in the middle of the night, the paralytic who was dropped down on his pallet through a hole in the roof, the woman who'd been hemorrhaging and only needed to touch his cloak to be healed. The centurion who came to him asking for his servant to be healed said, "Lord, I am not worthy to have you come under my roof, but only speak the word and my servant will be healed" (Matthew 8:8).

That's the attitude I find in the words, "Jesus Christ, have mercy upon me."

◆ ◆ ◆

So why the "miserable sinner" part? Why would I call myself a sinner in the middle of a prayer? Arthur Caliandro doesn't usually include that part of the prayer, as you might have noticed when I quoted him. For Arthur, who grew up the son of a Methodist minister, calling himself a sinner in the middle of prayer sends his imagination down the wrong path. It conjures up a stern, judgmental God, not the loving one he is praying to. I'm reminded of another friend who avoids the first verse of "Amazing Grace" because he hates singing "a wretch like me." "I'm not a wretch," he says, and he's not. He's a saintly man who washes pots at his church soup kitchen and visits patients in hospice care. I won't argue with him.

But I can tell you what I find helpful about those words. I'll give you two examples of people who have prayed them.

A man I'll call Joe made his living as a pickpocket. He'd worked with the best of the "light-fingered fraternity," and was proud of his skills. No pocket was safe, no safety clasp secure. He could remove a man's suspenders without the man feeling anything but a loss of support. His eyes were alert and busy, ferreting out marks, always on guard for police officers and plainclothes detectives.

Joe spent a few terms in prison and tried to go straight, working as a bellhop for a time, then a salesman, but he always returned to pickpocketing. With its lure of fast and easy money and its covert excitement, it was a sort of disease, an addiction. He'd notice a man patting his pocket, making sure the contents were safe—"fanning" it, in the pickpocket's lexicon—and the temptation would be too much for him. In a split second he'd have the wallet. Then he'd step back and watch the reaction. "I don't know whether I'd do this sort of thing because I was devilish or whether I wanted to satisfy my ego, but I did it," he wrote.

Life caught up with Joe. He rushed home to be at his dying father's bedside. A few years later it was his mother's bedside and funeral. Standing in the cemetery, he could see himself clearly. He was a thief, a sneak and felon. How could he have wandered so far from his mother's values? What a disappointment he must have been to her even if she never knew the full truth about him. The third time he rushed home was to be with his dangerously ill sister. Would he lose her too?

She recovered from emergency surgery but in her hospital bed she asked him to pray for her. He promised he would, and he did pray, but he reserved for himself the right to make a living the only way he knew how. He made a compromise with God, giving a percentage of his profits to the needy. "I was too much a con man to know that you don't make deals with God," he wrote.

Then Joe started to lose his touch. A large roll of money would slip from his grip. A wallet would be empty. Or he'd find himself surrounded by plainclothesmen. One day he lifted a fat wallet, opened it up and was stunned to find the most beautiful picture of Christ he had ever seen. Jesus' arms were outstretched on the cross and his expression was full of mercy and compassion. Joe looked at it in disbelief. He started to mumble over and over, "Jesus, have mercy on me, a sinner."

In the quiet of his room he knelt down and prayed, "O God, let thy will be done, not mine. Make me a better man. Give me strength to follow thy guidance. Let me be thy humble servant and serve thee well." The first thing he did when he got up was mail the wallet back to its owner.

He never stole again. Going straight was a constant struggle. That he did he saw as a credit to the power of prayer. He also prayed to be forgiven. "I know this is possible," he wrote, "because Jesus forgave Dismas, the thief on the cross."

The actor and songwriter Clifton Davis, author of the Jackson 5 hit "Never Can Say Good-bye" and star of the 1980s TV show *Amen* offers a different sort of example. He'd grown up a P.K.—a preacher's kid—was baptized and accepted Jesus into his life in a perfunctory way, but spiritually he was empty. Eventually he gave up on organized religion. He became an actor and moved to Hollywood. He was in a successful series and told himself he had made it, but inside he was deeply insecure. He took refuge in alcohol, then cocaine. By the late 1970s he was a habitual user.

His career went downhill. He sold his house in the Hollywood Hills and spent half the money on drugs. He sent his girlfriend packing because, in one of his few lucid moments, he realized he was actually a danger to her. She kept calling him, five or six times a day, pleading, "Don't snort those drugs. Talk to me." He'd slam down the phone. Finally he stopped answering it altogether.

By December 1980 he was drinking a quart of vodka a day and was down to skin and bones. At Christmas he decided he'd end his life. There was nothing left to live for. With his last thousand dollars he bought enough drugs to take an overdose.

While others in his apartment building were hanging wreaths and decorating trees, he got a hammer and nailed his apartment door shut. He didn't want anyone coming in and stopping him. He scrawled his will on a napkin and left it on a table.

All through Christmas Day he hunched on his bed, arms locked around his knees, preparing to take that final dose. The faint strains of carols like "Hark, the Herald Angels Sing" and "We Wish You a Merry Christmas" drifted in. The room darkened. Clifton's hurt grew unbearable. The phone rang. For a long time he wasn't even aware of it. Then something compelled him to pick up the receiver. It was his brother Carlyle. "Clifton?"

Clifton grunted.

"We're all worried about you," his brother went on. "Mama dreamed last night that you were dying."

Clifton started to hang up. His brother was a pastor and he didn't want to hear any preaching.

"The whole family is here," Carlyle said, "all your brothers and sisters. We are all so worried about you that none of us have opened our presents. We're having an all-night prayer meeting for you instead."

"Leave me alone," Clifton said.

"The Lord has given us the strong impression that we should keep on trying to let you know that God still loves you, that he wants you to live."

"What does God want with me anyway? There's nothing for me. I've seen it all, done it all. Why are you calling?"

"Brother, will you kneel down and pray with me?"

Steadying himself, Clifton knelt shakily on the floor. The only thing he could say was, "Lord, have mercy on me, a sinner."

Then he broke down and wept uncontrollably. He prayed in moans and groans. He felt unburdened of all those years of running away from God. He sensed Jesus standing right beside him and he knew without a doubt that Jesus had been standing by his side all along, just waiting for him.

"All right, Lord," he cried. "I surrender my life to you. Do with it what you will." As he lay on the cold floor, a gentle hand seemed to touch his head, and a warm peace filled him. He put the phone in the cradle. He felt no need for the cocaine. Somehow that night he left the apartment, got himself to the airport and caught a plane for Jacksonville, North Carolina, to be with his family.

With their support he freed himself from his drug dependency and recommitted himself to Christ. He went back to college, studied for the ministry and became ordained. He married the girlfriend who hadn't given up on him and they had a family. He took on the role in *Amen*, his life turned around.

*Jesus Christ, have mercy on me, a miserable sinner*... I'm not a pickpocket. I'm not a thief. I'm not a criminal. I've never been arrested. I'm not a drug abuser or a drunk. I've never felt such loss that I'm ready to close out the world and commit suicide. So what do I have in common with a pickpocket or an addict?

Nothing and everything. I can be arrogant, boastful, hardhearted, mean, stingy, unkind, cruel and selfish. Just because my sins seem subtler to the outside world doesn't mean they don't exist or aren't in some ways more pernicious because of their very murkiness. I would say that my worst sin, the sort of moral flaw that Jesus comes down hardest on, is my self-righteousness, the tape that plays inside my head telling me I'm better than others.

"Two men went up to the temple to pray," Jesus said, "one a Pharisee and the other a tax collector. The Pharisee, standing by himself, was praying thus: 'God, I thank you that I am not like other people: thieves, rogues, adulterers, or even like this tax collector. I fast twice a week. I give a tenth of all my income.' But the tax collector, standing far off, would not even look up to heaven, but was beating his breast and saying, 'God, be merciful to me, a sinner!' I tell you, this man went down to his home justified rather than the other; for all who exalt themselves will be humbled, but all who humble themselves will be exalted" (Luke 18:10–14).

Seems pretty clear to me where the most helpful attitude in prayer is. Bragging about being a sinner is not being humble. In fact, it can be downright tiresome. But praying with a sense of your sinfulness and failings is liberating. Reformed pickpockets and recovering addicts have a lot to offer people like me. The father loves the prodigal son's older brother, the one who stayed behind and did the right thing, just as much as he loves the wayward son. We're all God's children.

◆ ◆ ◆

One more thing about the Jesus Prayer: It's the easiest means I've ever found of satisfying that command of Paul's to pray without ceasing. There are times you need to think quite consciously about what you're praying. You need to do a moral inventory, an emotional self-exam. You need to come clean. There are other times when you just need to connect. God knows what's wrong, you don't, but if you could just get in touch you'd feel a lot better.

I'm not kidding when I say that I've prayed this one at work tons of times. I've prayed it often enough over the years that I don't have to concentrate on the words. I can simply flick the on switch and the prayer will be there. There is a lot of talk these days about multitasking. Quite frankly multitasking for me means doing several things at once and none of them well. I am best off if I'm one hundred percent present with the task at hand and that could mean sitting in a meeting and offering some insight, if I have an insight. But it means silencing the inner monologue. It means listening, paying attention, understanding.

To pray "Jesus Christ, have mercy on me, a miserable sinner. Make haste to help me, rescue me and save me, let thy will be done in my life" isn't adding a task to a multitasking day. It's taking away the needless tasks and distractions. It's asking God to be very present where we are. To use Kierkegaard's phrase, it is "to will one thing." To become a creature of hope and love, not fear. To encourage and not condemn, to trust and not flee.

A couple years ago I was in the back of an ambulance being whisked off to an ER, the EMTs hovering over me. I wasn't sure what was wrong with me, but the dark possibilities were endless: a stroke? A brain tumor? A seizure? An aneurysm? I'd been in the middle of a meeting with my colleagues when I realized I had no idea what anyone was saying. "Something's not right with my brain," I remember saying.

"We'll call Carol," they said. "What's your home number?"

I couldn't remember it.

They called 911 and they called Carol to meet me at the hospital. I was conscious of what was happening but couldn't understand what exactly was wrong. Stress would have been the best explanation, but I wasn't feeling especially stressed at the time. It was all very eerie.

As the ambulance sped through the streets of New York, I started praying the Jesus Prayer, the words circulating through my head. My racing pulse slowed down immediately. My fears were instantly allayed. My biggest concern was putting Carol through a harried trip to the ER. "You will be fine," came the message. Not that I was certain whether I would live or die, but I would be fine.

I was put on a gurney in the ER and got an MRI. Those machines make a racket, even through headphones, and to someone given to claustrophobia, as I am, they are no picnic. But my calm remained, and as I listened to the rattle of the machine I thought, "This has something to do with your dad dying." Somehow my body or my brain was reacting to a loss that it was still trying to process. As I write about it now, I feel myself wishing I could downplay the whole thing. What I don't want to do is diminish the comfort the Jesus Prayer gave me.

Five hours and a battery of tests later, I was released. I was fine. No seizure, no brain tumor, no stroke. All normal cognition returned. A follow-up trip to a neurologist revealed that, yes, I was fine. Did the prayer save me? Of course not. Did it reverse some dark scenario that was about to play itself out? I don't believe so. The medical explanation was something called Transient Global Amnesia, a brief episode of memory loss. Or at least that was the best diagnosis I could get out of any doctor and the usual poking around on the web.

The prayer had ministered to my fears. At a moment when I couldn't remember my own phone number I had no problem pulling up that prayer. It was right there ready to be used when I needed it most. Of course God was ready to help me. As I've said before, the words of a prayer aren't there for him as much as they are there for us. He hears us no matter what. But those words focused me on my relationship with God, my lifeline. "Jesus Christ, have mercy on me, a miserable sinner. Make haste to help me. Rescue me and save me. Let thy will be done in my life." With that I could trust.

## CHAPTER NINE

# Pray in Thanksgiving at All Times

*"Thanks."*

Mary Neal takes you by surprise. She's a doctor, an orthopedic surgeon, passionate and intense but very careful with her words, a rigorous thinker. She never exaggerates or embroiders a story. On the contrary, she works through the details with the care of an accountant going over a tax form. You know she's telling the truth, which makes it all the more compelling when she discusses something as numinous and insubstantial as the world beyond this one.

Her self-published memoir *To Heaven and Back* was an unexpected bestseller. And yet it was a book she put off writing for over ten years. She knew she had to tell her story but she had to mull over what to say, wanting to make sure she got it right. When she came by my office shortly after the book was published, I was impressed by her humility. She's fit and outdoorsy, with piercing blue eyes and a quiet voice. I can be wary of people who have had near-death experiences. I wonder how helpful their stories can be to those of us who haven't been so blessed. But Mary is a pragmatic person, and there was a message of thankfulness in her experience, thankfulness at the worst of times, that immediately spoke to me.

She and her husband, Bill, are experienced kayakers. When their four children were old enough to be left with a babysitter, they went on a vacation to the Chilean Andes to experience white-water kayaking in a remote corner of the globe, snow-fed rivers tumbling down volcanic slopes in subtropical terrain. Their guides were good friends, expert boaters.

That day in Chile towards the end of their week, Bill chose not to go out on the river. Mary started having second thoughts about going. There would be newer, less experienced kayakers joining the group and that made her uneasy, but Bill encouraged her to go. After all, this was the trip of a lifetime. She kissed her husband good-bye and headed off.

On the water, she hit trouble at the first drop. One of the novice kayakers got her boat lodged backwards going down the channel in front of Mary, and Mary had to navigate a more treacherous route. She took a deep breath and plunged fifteen, twenty feet down the falls. Her kayak dropped straight down. The paddle was ripped from her hands and the kayak smashed into some submerged rocks. Then it stopped.

She was trapped underwater, pinned by the sheer force of the waterfall above her, pushing her down. She couldn't move, couldn't release herself from the boat. Her body flopped in the vicious current like a rag doll. Fresh air was only a couple of feet above her but she couldn't reach it. She was stuck, unable to breathe, her kayak her coffin. As a doctor she assessed her situation and knew there was no hope. All she could do was pray. For a moment she fought mentally against her fate. She was terrified. Then she let go. *God*, she said, *thy will be done*.

Something in her shifted. The fear was gone and a great calm took over. No matter what happened, even if she died, even if she had to leave her husband and children, she knew everything would be okay. She was at peace, a sort of unexplainable heavenly peace, cosmic thankfulness beyond reason.

The current grabbed at her and jerked her body out of the kayak. Mary the orthopedic surgeon took notice as though she were her own patient: "Your knee bones just broke . . . You just tore your ligaments . . ."

At the same moment, with a *pop*, her soul rose from her body. She shot up above the river into another realm. Fifteen or twenty spirits rushed forward to welcome her. They hugged her and danced with her. Though their outlines were blurry, she knew that she knew them and that they were sent by God. "I couldn't identify each by name as, for instance, my dead grandfather or my old babysitter," she said, "but I knew each of them well."

With the spirits she began to glide along a path. She was going home, heading to her eternal home. Her companions could barely contain their joy, joy at her death. A feeling of absolute love pierced her, a feeling greater than anything she'd ever known. Below her, Mary could see her body on the riverbank, the shell of an old friend.

On the riverbank, Mary's earthly friends were giving her CPR, desperately trying to bring her back to life. "Breathe, Mary, breathe," they cried. She loved them and didn't want them to be sad so she flew back to take a breath, then continued on her heavenly journey with her spiritual companions.

They headed to a great hall with an immense dome and a central arch built with shimmering gold blocks. She was flooded with a longing to be reunited with God. Still, her friends on earth beckoned, and she returned to take another breath, and another, before continuing her journey.

At the gate of heaven her companions revealed to her that it wasn't her time to enter. "You have more to do on earth," she was told. Sorrow filled her but she knew she had to go back, back to life. She opened her eyes on the riverbank to see the stunned faces of her friends, thankful that she was alive.

She and Bill had a long, exhausting trip flying back to their home in Jackson Hole, Wyoming. She almost died a second time en route and was perilously close to death when she was finally hospitalized.

She woke up to see two deacons from church. They brought her some outdoor magazines to read and she remembered thinking that as nice as it was to see her friends, she really wanted to read the magazines. She had no pain and her mind was clear.

But as soon as her friends left and Mary picked up the magazines, the pages became too blurry to read. She put them down and turned on the TV. It was too blurry to watch. Even the face of the nurse who came in later was a blur. After a nap Mary asked for a Bible and picked it up, looking for verses to guide her. Maybe she could find one of her favorite psalms for reassurance. But those words were a blur. She couldn't grasp the meaning of any sentences.

Mary was about to give up in frustration and put the book aside, when she turned to 1 Thessalonians. One verse became clear: "Rejoice always." What a reminder that joy was a choice, not something based on circumstances but what came from a willingness to focus on hope and the promises of God.

Then another verse became visible: "Pray without ceasing." Prayer was the way to communicate directly with God, listening for his guidance. She'd just had an extraordinary experience of prayer, praying at the moment of death, "Thy will be done" and through prayer she saw where her soul would take her when her body was gone. Paul's advice to pray without ceasing landed on very willing ears. Prayer was the only way to understand what had happened to her.

Finally a third verse became clear: "Give thanks in all circumstances, for this is the will of God in Christ Jesus for you."

Give thanks in all things, in all circumstances, even in this. Give thanks for this life even when the next life promised indescribable joy. Give thanks through the pain of recovery and all that she was still meant to do on earth.

For the next several days the rest of the Bible remained blurry, magazines proved impossible to read, people's faces—even her loved ones'—were unrecognizable. But these three verses were crystal clear. Three verses that summarize what God asks of us and what we can do.

◆ ◆ ◆

Of all the means of prayer, gratitude is one of the easiest. Even people who are not particularly faithful can choose gratitude. At Thanksgiving at our house we usually go around the dinner table and each person mentions something they're grateful for: good health, great kids, a winning soccer team, the food on our plates, the presidential election, a passing grade in chemistry. Other virtues can be so much harder to acquire. Tell yourself to be hopeful and if you're worried sick and biting your fingernails it's not going to change your thinking. Tell yourself to be patient and after ten minutes at baggage claim at the airport, looking for your green suitcase among all the black ones, you will be fuming. But "let gratitude be your attitude" is one of those pithy sayings you can actually make happen. It doesn't take much to train your mind to be grateful. A pen and paper will do.

Several years ago I worked with newscaster Deborah Norville on an article about gratitude. In her three decades as a TV reporter, she observed, "I've always marveled that certain people, even in the face of heart-stopping obstacles and the most difficult circumstances, are able to go forward with smiles on their faces and optimism in their outlooks. How is that possible? In each instance, it comes down to the same answer: They were grateful."

Deborah believes in actually writing down what you are grateful for, keeping track of your blessings in a journal the way you keep track of your checks in your checkbook. She insists it's good for your career, your family life, your marriage, your well-being, and she offered scientific research to prove it. Studies have shown a measurable increase in health, resilience, cognitive skills and the ability to undo stress through gratitude. She pointed out the work of two professors in particular, Robert Emmons and Michael McCullough.

In one experiment they took three groups of volunteers and randomly assigned them to focus on one of three things for a week: hassles, things for which they were grateful, or ordinary life events. The people who focused on gratitude were happier. They reported fewer negative physical symptoms and were active in healthy ways. They spent almost an hour and a half more per week exercising than the people who focused on their hassles.

Deborah told me about how she used gratitude to combat a health problem. "For years I've suffered migraines," she said. "I've done everything every doctor recommended, but after my investigation into gratitude I tried something new. I made a daily habit of writing down the things that made me grateful. And I started seeing the benefits. My migraines have all but disappeared, my energy has increased and I've experienced joy by 'being there' for others."

She called it "Thank You Power" and wrote a book with the same name. Her prescription: Write down three things every day that you're thankful for. Three things was all, duly noted and recorded. "You need to work on it consciously to make a difference," she said.

Her advice made sense though I was certain it wasn't anything I needed to follow. I'm a natural optimist. Why did I need to write down what I was thankful for? If I just felt grateful, wasn't that enough? I had plenty of ways to pray. I could sing or talk to God or use the Jesus Prayer. To have to write things down seemed so artificial. Couldn't I be like Mary Neal and just read Paul's advice to the Thessalonians?

To give thanks in all circumstances would be just like going around the Thanksgiving table (note I hadn't really taken in the "in all circumstances" part). To thank the cook who made the meal and then the grocer who supplied the ingredients would lead back to God who gave the sun and the rain and the soil that made the food grow.

Oh, writer beware.

Yes, thankfulness is something you can put into practice even when you're not feeling it. Doing so offers all sorts of lifestyle benefits, but sometimes thankfulness is the only way you can pray and to do it at the worst of times is to acquire an invaluable tool of faith, startling because it seems so counterintuitive. Prayers like "Noooooooooo!" and "Help me, God" and "My heart's breaking" or "I feel like shouting for joy" are just what comes out of us at the moment. "Thanks" can take work but the work is everything.

Before I share my own story of thankfulness, let me tell you two others.

◆ ◆ ◆

For two years after her divorce Sheryl Smith-Rodgers's teenage son, Patrick, didn't speak to her. He chose to stay with his father and didn't even say good-bye when she moved out of the house. He barely spoke when she called. He blocked her e-mails. He ignored her invitations to come over for sloppy joes, his favorite. Occasionally she'd catch a glimpse of him driving his pickup around their small Texas town or she'd see him at the feed store where he worked.

One afternoon, fed up with the blocked e-mails and ignored calls, Sheryl drove to the feed store and climbed into the passenger seat of Patrick's unlocked pickup truck to wait for him. When Patrick came out and saw her his expression turned sour. He slid behind the wheel and said, "Can you get out, please?"

"Can't we talk?" she pleaded.

"I'm going to say it once more—please get out, Mother." She shook her head.

"Then do me a favor," Patrick said, "and lock both doors before you leave." He slid back out and slammed the door.

The pain of it was unbearable. She and Patrick had been so close when he was young. She missed him so much, hated being locked out of his life. On the Sunday before Thanksgiving her pastor had preached on the text from 1Thessalonians, the same one that inspired Mary Neal—"In everything give thanks"—but Sheryl didn't know how she could do it. How could she be grateful if her son wouldn't be joining her for the holiday?

"Instead of asking God for things you want," the minister had said, "try thanking him for what he's given you."

Thanksgiving morning Sheryl forced herself to do just that. She'd focus on the good things she'd been given. She was thankful that Patrick was doing well in school. That he worked hard and had close friends. That he was healthy and that she'd had so much time with him when he was young. Before she even got out of bed, she thanked God for her house, for another day, for her daughter, for her parents, with whom they would be spending Thanksgiving. And she thanked God for her son.

Later that morning she found a stack of greeting cards and wrote in a blank one: "I love you more than you can ever imagine. Always. Happy Thanksgiving!" Then on her way to dinner with her parents, she dropped by the feed store.

Patrick looked tired, stressed, stacking some feed bags. She kept it low-key. "Here," she said, handing him the card. "Happy Thanksgiving!" He opened it up and read. Was there a hint of a smile on his face? Did he open up just a little? "Tell Grandma and Grandpa hello for me," he said. Sheryl nodded and waved and got back in the car.

She stuck with her morning prayers of gratitude and thanked God for little things throughout the day. She opened up a new e-mail account and wrote Patrick chatty little notes. She ended each with "I love you, Mom." Was he reading them? She had no clue. At least he wasn't blocking them.

A few weeks later he showed up at her door. "Can I come in?" he asked.

"Of course," she said. They talked about school, his girlfriend, work. He even agreed to come over for sloppy joes. Then he started showing up for dinner once a week. On his eighteenth birthday she hosted a birthday party for him (sloppy joes were on the menu, of course). Her son was back in her life.

I generally avoid using the phrase "prayer works." In the Bible the operative word is more often that God "answers" prayer or God "hears" our prayers, different from the quid-pro-quo notion that "prayer works." The prayer that works best for you might not be the one you expect, the way God hears you might not be how you think.

Sheryl's greatest hopes were realized when she expressed gratitude for what she already had, not for what she fervently wished for. God answered her prayer "Please bring Patrick back to me" when she took a leap of faith. Maybe it was all a matter of time. Perhaps Patrick would have resumed talking to her anyway. But I suspect the change in her attitude was what made their reunion possible. Her prayerful response to a painful situation changed the situation. It changed her, changed her expectations. Give thanks for everything? Well, yes. Everything.

◆ ◆ ◆

The second story is far more dramatic and doesn't offer the happy ending that Sheryl's does, but perhaps it's worth remembering that the author of 1 Thessalonians was frequently writing from prison and by his own account, in his second letter to the Corinthians, was beaten, stoned, shipwrecked, adrift at sea, threatened by bandits, hungry, thirsty, cold, exhausted. If the Apostle Paul could be thankful in all circumstances, he knew just how difficult that could be. And how necessary.

Chet Bitterman Jr. was in the middle of an Amazon jungle at the graveside of his twenty-eight-year-old son and clinging to thankfulness as his very lifeline. He told himself to be thankful that it wasn't raining that day, that the location was beautiful, that his wife was with him, that his son's short life had been lived for a larger purpose.

His son, also named Chet, had gone to Colombia to work with Wycliffe Bible Translators, an organization that has translated the Bible into hundreds of languages that had never been written down before. Young Chet would be in a tribal area working with the native people. His wife had flown to Bogotá for a week for a medical check when the Wycliffe house where they were staying was invaded by armed guerrillas. They took one hostage, Chet III. The price for his return: the withdrawal of all Wycliffe workers in Colombia.

Back in Pennsylvania Chet the father raged. He paced the house, up to the kitchen, back to the basement. He was a man of action, the head of a small business. While his wife called endless organizations, asking for prayers, Chet wanted to do something. He'd get some guns and with his buddies, fly to Bogotá and take the place apart, brick by brick, until they found his son.

Of course it was a fantasy, but he needed some outlet for his rage. "Lord," he prayed, "there's got to be something I can do."

*There is. Give thanks.*

The thought came out of nowhere and it wouldn't go away. *Give thanks.* Unlike his missionary son, Chet hadn't learned hundreds of Bible verses by heart, but this one he knew: "In every thing give thanks: for this is the will of God . . ."

He argued and protested. Give thanks for his son's kidnapping? The pointlessness of it, the stupidity made him want to throw something. He felt shocked, angry, frustrated—anything but thankful. Then he noticed that the verse didn't say anything about how you felt. "Give thanks" was the command, not "feel thankful." Thanksgiving was a matter not of the emotions but of the will.

He wanted justice, he wanted revenge, but as he paced, he forced himself to do what seemed utterly unnatural. He would be honest. Where could he start?

Well, he would be thankful for all those Bible verses his son could recite. They must have been helpful. And thankful that Chet III was young and strong and in such good shape. He took out a piece of paper and began writing things down. Thank God that his son spoke fluent Spanish. Thank God that he made friends easily. Thank God that he had called only two days earlier and had such a good talk with his mother.

As he wrote, the tension and rage and anguish drained away. He felt light, free... thankful. Feelings that he could never have drummed up by straining for them had come through an act of obedience.

The kidnappers' deadline was one month away. Then it got extended two weeks. Chet and his wife, Mary, grew hopeful. Surely their son would be released. At no point did they suggest that Wycliffe capitulate to the kidnappers' demands. That could endanger Wycliffe workers all over the world. Rumors flared, but he had to believe that his son was still alive. They had to trust.

Less than two months after the kidnapping, the terrible news came: Chet Bitterman III was dead, his body found in an abandoned bus on a side street in Bogotá.

The next few days passed in a blur. Sympathy from friends at church. A letter from the president. More news from Colombia and then the burial in a jungle clearing near the Wycliffe base.

When life came back into focus for Chet, it was from a different angle, a new one for him, "the view from forever," as he called it. He would still struggle with his tragedy, still object to the senselessness of his son's death, but he had a tool to cling to. The key to seeing as God does is to give thanks in everything. He could stand by his son's grave with love, not anger. He could forgive the horror that had been done. He could look forward. Prayer had given him a new perspective, giving thanks when he felt anything but thankful.

◆ ◆ ◆

Am I thankful that I had open-heart surgery? Of course. I am thankful to the doctors, thankful that someone figured out I had an aneurysm before it ruptured, thankful to the nurses who took such good care of me. Without surgery I would not be alive. But here's something a little harder to explain: I'm thankful for the compassion it's given me for anyone else who goes through the trials of major surgery. Especially the recovery.

Four weeks out of surgery, I crashed. I felt rotten. I would lie in bed shivering under a mountain of quilts, close my eyes in the hope of sleep, and what came to me was a small dark block in my head. Imagine all your deepest fears pressed down and packed together into a domino that's lodged in your head. You can't step around it, you can't ignore it, you can feel its brooding presence and you wonder if it will explode or suck you into endless night. I could almost locate it near my forehead. I started calling it the black domino, all dark blankness and not a single dot of light.

I had asked my cardiologist about my chances of sinking into depression. It's a well-known side effect of open-heart surgery. Some call it pump head, blaming it on the heart-lung machine that takes over for your heart during surgery. Others suggest it's the result of confronting mortality.

"I don't think depression will be a problem for you," Dr. Ravalli said cautiously. "You're in good shape. You'll be recovering at home with your family. Depression isn't as much a problem as it used to be. Do you normally get depressed?"

"No," I said confidently. I'm more prone to anxiety than depression. Depressives tend to look backward at their lives, shaking their heads with regret, remembering all the "could have beens" and "would have beens," the "if I only." My head doesn't fly that way. I'm more likely to be looking forward, worrying, wondering, "Can I?" or "Will I" or "What if I don't?"

I lay in bed, watching the black domino warily, monitoring it like the enemy. It *was* the enemy. Was I going to plunge into a bottomless pit of gloom? Was I going off the deep end? I could count on one hand the few times in my life when I'd brushed against something that felt like depression, nothing close to the paralyzing depression I've seen others suffer.

I remembered an August day before my junior year of college. I had spent the summer backpacking around Europe on a fifteen-dollar-a-day budget. It was near the end of my trip and I was sitting on a hill in an Edinburgh park on a languid afternoon, incapable of moving. I'd either traveled too much or seen too many old paintings or believed too little that I didn't want to do anything for weeks on end. I couldn't bear to visit another museum or castle or church or town square or sleep in another youth hostel or bed and breakfast. It all seemed purposeless and I figured if I stayed on that patch of Scottish grass all night, no one would really care. I could die there and it wouldn't matter. I was overcome with a kind of lassitude that only the young, with their boundless energy, can ever know.

I slept for hours and when I awoke saw only my failures, which appeared as numberless as the stars in the sky. What an insignificant person I was, what a terrible fake. In the dark I finally shook off my torpor, got up and got something to eat, returning to the dreary dorm room I had rented. For a long while that was my benchmark for depression. I could tell myself, "I don't want to go there," and managed through some combination of exercise, prayer, optimism and genetic good fortune to stay away.

Till now with this black domino lodged in my brain, this black hole that threatened to absorb everything.

Was it claustrophobia? I hate being in closed spaces. In my editorial career there is only one story that gave me the creeps so much I couldn't work on it. It was about a man who went scuba diving through Caribbean coral caves and came to a spot that got narrower and narrower until he couldn't get out. He couldn't turn around and he couldn't figure out the route that would take him back. His air was running out. Through the murky water and the coral he could see sunlight above but couldn't reach it.

Fortunately for him, he was able to escape, but that remains my worst nightmare. To be trapped. Maybe my body was still objecting to being strapped down on a hospital bed for hours of surgery, a machine doing the work of my heart and lungs.

"But you're doing all the right things," I told myself. I walked around the small park near our house three times a day. I took naps. I ate carefully, filling myself up with protein and iron. I had oatmeal for breakfast and lentil soup for lunch. I took prescription painkillers when I had to. Otherwise two Advil at bedtime and another two in the middle of the night.

"I'm not getting better," I told Carol.

"Give it some time," she said. "It's not going to be a straightforward trajectory. You'll have good days and some bad days—a few steps forward, a few steps back—but you'll feel better over the long term."

No reason why that shouldn't happen. But I couldn't believe it and I felt myself unalterably changed. The novelty of being a patient had worn off. The adrenaline of surgery was long gone. I was in the deep slough of recovery and I hated it. Like that scuba diver in the Caribbean trapped in his coral cave, I could see the light of day but it was agonizingly out of reach. And when I closed my eyes I could still see the black domino.

I couldn't pray. I couldn't reach God. He was that light above me. I could accept that he was there but I couldn't get to him. This time it wasn't enough to tell myself that others were praying for me and doing it on my behalf. Not anymore.

"You should keep a positive attitude," I told myself. I'd read about how positive thinking could help you bounce back from surgery and help in your recovery. But I couldn't force myself to be positive and that made me feel even more like a failure. If you're not positive, you're not going to get better. "Thanks a lot," I wanted to say. Couldn't I be angry that I felt awful? Why couldn't I express my anger to God?

I picked up my battered volume of the New Testament and Psalms and complained, "I'm mad at you, God." I read from a psalm (3:7) that was full of rage: "Arise, O Lord; save me, O my God, for thou has smitten all mine enemies upon the cheek bone; thou hast broken the teeth of the ungodly." I thought it could get me in touch with my anger. But it didn't make me feel any better.

I turned to the cheery brochure that was supposed to guide us in our recovery. If my temperature shot up to 102, then I was supposed to take myself to the ER. If the dull pain in my chest became a dagger, call 911. If my incision began to puff up and ooze, I should call my surgeon. Otherwise I was to keep up the walking, the stretching, eating three meals a day, sleeping at regular hours. No lifting groceries. No driving. Light dusting was okay and vacuuming but no pushing heavy furniture around or reaching up to wash the windows. There was nothing in there about the black domino.

Maybe I had PTSD. The surgery itself is traumatic. Your sternum has been sawed open—"stretched," in my surgeon's euphemistic words. Your body has been chilled in surgery. You had all that anesthesia. You were strapped down and put out, then cut open and wired shut. Is it any wonder that some part of you reacts by declaring, "Don't do that again!"? My head was trying to defend against anything so violent happening to my body again. The shell-shocked soldier who comes back from war, who hits the deck at the backfiring of a car, requires countless hours of therapy to feel right with the world again.

I searched the brochure for some evidence that that's what I was going through. No mention of this nightmare.

"Do you have a fever?" Carol asked, watching me shiver.

"I don't know. I haven't taken my temperature."

"Are you hot?"

"I'm cold."

"You could call the doctor."

"The brochure says you don't need to call the doctor unless you have a fever of 102. Mine's not that high."

"How do you know?"

I got out the old gray thermometer that we used for the kids and stuck it in my mouth until it bleeped. I showed Carol the evidence just to prove that I wasn't that sick: 100.4. High enough to feel bad but not so alarming as to rush to the hospital or call the doctor. I was tired of being a patient, weary of finding myself in a narrative that had no clear middle or end. Open-heart surgery was a story, something to write home about. Surgery was a crisis moment when everyone could pray and send me e-mails. There was nothing to say about the muddle of recovery. What do you say about a fever that was only 100.4?

"You've talked about wanting to have a sabbatical someday," Carol said, looking for the upside. "Maybe you can think of this time as your sabbatical."

A nice thought, but not one I could put into practice. On the ideal sabbatical my head would be clear enough so that I could read through Proust and Tolstoy and Dante, savoring the greats with the greatest mental agility. I wasn't up to that. I watched old videos and thumbed my way through the books friends had sent me.

I was a dead weight. I couldn't clean the house or give a dinner party or even do the laundry. About the only challenge I was up for was writing a thank-you note. That I could try. "Just the kind of thing Deborah Norville would have you do," I thought. I'd e-mailed her shortly after surgery, just to tell her what I was going through. She'd responded with a generous prayer. But her "thank-you power" advice? That was still on file somewhere in my head.

I sat on the side of my bed and took out a note card. I looked over at the gifts people had sent. There was a bowl my coworker Celeste had given me for my oatmeal, the perfect thing. But why write her? I would see her soon enough back at the office. I could say something then. She wouldn't be expecting anything from me.

No, I needed to write it down now, all my gratitude. I would forget it in a couple of days. I scrawled a few sentences. At once there was an inner *ping*, as sure as the clanging of a bell: "Yes, that's right. That's you, Rick. That's who you are. That's where you want to be." I was hungry to be grateful, desperate like a starving man seeking food or a thirsty one crawling across the desert for water. It was almost physical, holding a pen in my hand and opening a blank card, my mind looking for words to describe a kindness. Thankfulness was the one thing that would keep the black domino from sucking me up and absorbing me. Thankfulness expressed in very specific terms.

I wrote another note and another. Thank you for the card, thanks for the roses, thanks for the burritos from FreshDirect, thanks for the bottle of wine, thanks for the friendship, thanks for the postcard that made me laugh, thanks for the CD, thanks for the phone call, thanks for the prayers, thanks for the visit, thanks for the e-mail.

I could hear myself as I wrote. I could feel stirrings of faith even if I was writing nothing about my faith because I was participating again in the goodness of the world. Sitting on the side of my bed and writing was my therapy. Later at church someone said, "I can't believe you sent me a note thanking me for my note." How could I say that the note I sent her was vital to my recovery?

Prayer *is* communication and this was essential communication. Our friend F. Paul had sent me a slew of witty postcards over the last month, every one of them a gem. One day I picked out a dozen of them and made a silly collage of the images to send to him as thanks. Back at ya. I couldn't pray the way I was accustomed to, but writing thank-you notes—something so mundane and yet so profound—was my prayer. I could connect to my spiritual core. I could do battle against the inner darkness pulling me down. I could linger in the light.

In a matter of weeks I sent seventy-five thank-you notes and post-cards. I hope I never have to read them. I'm sure they were inane or over-the-top or even illegible. But they were a godsend to me. I could wait, pen in hand, and tell myself, "I don't really have anything to say," but once I started writing, all sorts of things came out. Gratitude wasn't far beneath the surface. It was just waiting to be expressed. I'm amazed that I actually had seventy-five different people to write, seventy-five people who did nice things for me. But once you start looking for things to be grateful for, you end up feeling grateful in the most cosmic way.

For me it was a way to reclaim the turf I longed to inhabit and it kept me from sinking into godless despair. It was many months before the black domino disappeared—I can still conjure it up like a phantom in a Stephen King novel. But I had found the tool to banish it, one I still use.

Be thankful in all things. Write them down. Even if you don't feel grateful, even if you can't pray. What you write will be your prayer. Feelings you can't force, faith is not something you can necessarily talk yourself into, but thankfulness you can. All it takes is a pen or a pencil and a scrap of paper. You can write to yourself, you can write to a friend, you can write to God. Put your gratitude down, even at the worst of times. Especially then. What you say will lift you back up.

## CHAPTER TEN

# Pray Yes

---

*"Yes, and . . . "*

For Tim's graduation from high school, some intrepid parent, who happened to be a TV producer, talked comedian Tina Fey into being the guest speaker. She was short even in heels, pretty, gracious, funny and visibly nervous at the prospect of delivering an inspiring talk to a bunch of teens.

Her comedic background had been in improvisational theater and she used the rules of improv as a jumping-off point to explain how to get the most out of life. One of those rules was "Yes, and . . . "

Her point was that when you're doing improv and someone says something like, "What a fine horse you were riding this morning," you don't say, "That wasn't a horse! It was an elephant, you idiot." You go with whatever they said and build on it. "Yes, and did you know that I'm using it to train for the Olympics this summer to win another gold medal in dressage?" or "Yes, and we just came from a cowboy breakfast on the ranch" or "Yes, and it's the horse my grandfather gave me for my twenty-first birthday." "Yes, and…" instead of "No, but…"

She wanted the graduates to be open to life's possibilities, to make the most of the opportunities that God had presented them and *would* present to them. "Yes, and…" means seeing people in a positive, generous light, listening closely to what they were saying and loving them. "Yes, and…" would require chipping away at the walls of cynicism and defensiveness. "Yes, and…" would be a worldview of imagination and creativity. Instead of saying "I couldn't possibly do that," you might find you can do more than you ever thought possible when you say "Yes, and…"

Sitting under the sycamores in dappled shade, listening to Tina Fey, I felt like she was speaking to me as much as to the graduates in their caps and gowns. What was my knee-jerk response to the internal nudges of charity, generosity, adventure? "No, God, I couldn't do that" or "Yes, and what else did you have in mind and how can you help me accomplish it?" Couldn't I live a little more dangerously? The Bible is full of occasions when Jesus seemed to be looking for a "Yes, and…" and got a No instead.

Take the rich young man who came to Jesus and asked what good deed he should do to earn eternal life. What if he hadn't walked away at the answer? Jesus' first response was to tell him to keep the commandments. "Which ones?" the young man asked. Jesus went through the familiar litany (in case the fellow was clueless): you shall not murder, you shall not commit adultery, you shall not steal, you shall not bear false witness, honor your father and mother.

Smugly—you can hear the self-satisfaction—the young man said, "I have kept all these. What do I still lack?" Jesus answered: "Go, sell your possessions and give to the poor and you will have treasure in heaven. Then, come follow me" (Matthew 19:16).

What if the young man had said "Yes, and...?" What if his answer were even as equivocal as "Yes, Lord, I want to follow you but it's a big step for me and I need your help"? Instead he walked away, "grieving," in the Bible's damning phrase, "for he had many possessions."

We Americans, by any reckoning of the world's resources, have many possessions. What would we have said? If that guy had stuck around just a little bit longer he might have heard Jesus give a more hopeful prognosis. No, the rich didn't have a chance. After all, it is easier for a camel to go through the eye of a needle than for a rich man to enter the kingdom of heaven. Yet "for mortals it is impossible, but for God all things are possible."

"Yes, and..."

Not too many years ago Elizabeth Sherrill was writing at her computer at home, struggling to meet a deadline, when she heard a rustling in the woods outside. At the edge of the trees she caught sight of a skunk zigzagging across the lawn. What was that on his head? A bizarre-looking helmet: a yellow plastic yogurt container. Like a drunk he whirled in one direction and then another, bumping against the picnic table in the backyard, shaking his head frantically. But the container was wedged tight.

Tibby wasn't about to go out there and take the yogurt container off. How would she ever catch the skunk? It would take too long.

What if she got sprayed? The odor was impossible to get rid of. But she couldn't get the skunk out of her mind.

She called the SPCA and was told to call the Department of Wildlife. There the man listened to her story. He put her on hold, talked to someone else in the office, let her know that if the skunk couldn't see her, he wouldn't spray. She could take off the carton and then throw a blanket over the skunk just in case, letting it amble out when she was at a safe distance.

Tibby glanced outside. No more skunk. She was off the hook. Surely the animal was long gone by now. Someone else would find it. They'd get a conservation officer who could handle the problem.

Still, as soon as she hung up the phone she went outside. No blanket, no special strategy. "My feet never slowed," she wrote. "I turned left and dashed down the street as though rushing to a long-ordained appointment." She'd gotten a hundred yards down the road when a black-and-white streak emerged from the bushes and ran straight at her, the yellow helmet on his head.

She stooped and grabbed hold of the yogurt container. The animal tugged and twisted. She had to grab it with both of her hands and tug—until a small black head popped free. "A sharp quivering nose, two small round ears and alert black eyes stared straight into mine," she wrote.

For a full ten seconds they held each other's gaze. Then the skunk turned and vanished into a culvert.

She hadn't wanted to get involved. She was busy after all. Why bother? She could have justified not going outside, leaving this problem in the capable hands of some professional. Instead she tried and it worked, and for years afterward she kept that plastic yogurt container on her desk as a reminder that "every now and then God's answer to a need is me." Something had to be done and that something involved her.

Prayer might seem like a quiet, contemplative thing. It is, but it is also an action to take. Jesus spent forty days in the wilderness, praying and fasting, before he launched his ministry. Even then he was frequently leaving the crowd and going off by himself to be alone to pray, but the narrative of the Gospels is an account of exhausting activity. He healed the sick, raised the dead, fed the hungry with loaves and fishes, made the lame walk and the blind see, preached, exhorted, taught and blessed. In John's phrase, there were so many "other things that Jesus did; if every one of them were written down, I suppose that the world itself could not contain the books that would be written" John 21:25. To pray and to act. A prayer can inspire an act but the act can be the prayer itself.

Kevin Felts is a freelance cameraman who was hired to film a famous Oregon author for a documentary. Part of the shoot involved going back to the house the author had lived in before his unexpected fame, when times were tough for him. The father of six, he was working three jobs and barely making ends meet back then.

The house looked very familiar to Kevin. It reminded him of a Christmas not long before when he wanted to make a gift to someone in his community. He'd come through some tough times and knew what it was like to face the holidays in diminished circumstances.

Now that things were going well he wanted to pass along his good fortune. He'd heard of a family that needed help. He didn't know their name and didn't want to. He put a hundred dollars in an envelope and slipped it in under their door. Not that it would solve all their problems, but it might give them hope. He'd had this urge to give and had acted on it.

And now Kevin was looking at the same house.

Kevin told the famous author the story about the cash in the envelope, what he'd heard about the family of eight needing help, how he'd done the whole thing anonymously and put the money under the door.

The author was amazed. Yes, he said, he was the one who'd picked up the envelope. In fact, the gift of a hundred dollars had come at just the right time. He'd been working on a book, something he'd written just for his family, the amazing story of a man finding faith at the hardest, saddest, toughest point of his life. He'd finished a draft of the novel, but didn't have any money to make copies of it. Then came the unexpected hundred.

"I had fifteen copies of it printed up at Office Depot," the author said, "and gave the book away. If I hadn't had that money I probably would never have shared it." He might never have been urged to pass it along, might never have decided to publish it.

That book, *The Shack*, went on to sell some fifteen million copies and became an international phenomenon for the author, Paul Young. Of course, it is entirely possible that some other form of good fortune would have come Paul's way. *The Shack* might have found its way to the public through some other means. Or maybe Paul would have gotten a lucrative full-time job and put the manuscript into a drawer to be forgotten for years. But look at what an anonymous gift did when it came at just the right time. Kevin said, "Yes, and..." Moreover he got to find out what actually happened when he acted.

For years I've saved a prayer that was a favorite of Eleanor Roosevelt's. According to her son Elliott, she said it every night before she went to bed:

*Our Father, who has set a restlessness in our hearts and made us all seekers after that which we can never fully find, forbid us to be satisfied with what we make of life. Draw us from base content and set our eyes on far-off goals. Keep us at tasks too hard for us that we may be driven to thee for strength. Deliver us from fretfulness and self-pitying; make us sure of the good we cannot see and of the hidden good in the world. Open our eyes to simple beauty all around us and our hearts to the loveliness men hide from us because we do not try to understand them. Save us from ourselves and show us a vision of a world made new.*

I am especially fond of the phrase "keep us at tasks too hard for us that we may be driven to thee for strength." If there was ever someone who took on difficult tasks, it was Eleanor Roosevelt, especially when you consider some of the emotional challenges she had to overcome.

Shy, awkward, ungainly, bookish, she was born to wealth and status, the niece of a president, but what a tragic childhood. Her mother, a great beauty, died when Eleanor was eight; her father, a terrible alcoholic, died two years later. I remember one story from her girlhood when she was accompanying her father to his club. He left her in a downstairs room, "the dogs' room" as it was called, to get a quick drink. Hours later, Eleanor waiting all the while, he was carried back down, passed out. As a friend pointed out, "No wonder she couldn't bear being with anyone who drank." She was so serious a child her society mother called her Granny, which must have only confirmed her low self-worth; then when she married the handsome, charismatic Franklin, she spent years sharing the same house with his doting, demanding mother. Later she had to cope with the heartbreaking evidence of his infidelity.

And yet her passion for the oppressed and the poor drove her beyond her insecurities, fueling her. By the time she was First Lady she led an exhausting schedule of speeches, newspaper columns, press conferences, dinners, lunches, trips to the front lines, meetings with the unemployed. She was an advocate for civil rights, famously inviting the black contralto Marian Anderson to sing at the Lincoln Memorial when she had been blocked from performing at Constitution Hall. After the war, she was America's delegate to the UN, chairing the committee that created the Universal Declaration of Human Rights.

Historian Mary Ann Glendon took those last words from the prayer—"a world made new"—as the title of her book on Eleanor Roosevelt's key role in the human rights movement. It is the nature of the inner life that it leaves fewer documents behind of its workings, especially compared to the clamor of political wrangling and daily news. Only God knows exactly what petitions Eleanor added to her bedside prayer, but her actions show evidence of her prayer at work.

"Courage is fear that has said its prayers," goes an old saying. It is not that the courageous have fewer fears than the rest of us but that they move beyond them. They say, "Yes, and..." despite their insecurity and fears.

Bob Macauley founded the relief organization AmeriCares, distributing medicine and medical supplies to the world's poor at times of disaster. They've given billions of dollars of aid to more than 135 countries in thirty years. Bob himself was a terrific fundraiser, going hat in hand to the CEOs of some of the biggest corporations but as he said, he learned how to beg from the very best.

Back in the early days of AmeriCares, when Bob was still trying to grow the organization and wondering how on earth he could get the means to fund his vision, he was on a trip visiting orphanages in Guatemala with the diminutive and tireless Mother Teresa. Bob was tall and strapping and Mother Teresa less than five feet. He showed me a picture of the two of them walking on the tarmac at some airport, his hand at her back.

"You seem to be giving Mother Teresa a hand," people would say when they saw the photo.

"Not at all," Bob insisted. "I've got my hand on her back to slow her down. I couldn't keep up!"

The two of them were on a Taca Airlines flight from Guatemala to Mexico City. The flight attendant brought them their lunches.

"Excuse me," Mother Teresa said, "how much does this meal cost?" A question Bob was pretty sure no passenger had ever asked.

The flight attendant shrugged. "I don't know. About one dollar in US currency."

"If I give it back to you," Mother Teresa said, "would you give me that dollar to give to the poor?"

The flight attendant looked startled. "I don't know," she stammered. "It's not something we normally do." She left her cart, went to the front of the plane to consult the pilot, then returned. "Yes, Mother," she said. "You may have the money for the poor."

"Here then," Mother Teresa handed back the tray. No matter how hungry he might have been, Bob did the same. No way was he going to be able to eat in peace with Mother Teresa seated next to him. As it turned out, the rest of the passengers on the plane followed suit. The flight attendant got on the speaker and announced, "If anyone gives up their meal, the airline will give one dollar to Mother Teresa for the poor." It seemed no one wanted to eat their lunch. Bob got up and counted: 129 people gave up their lunches, including the crew.

"Pretty good," he said to Mother Teresa, "now you've got one hundred and twenty-nine dollars for the poor."

But she wasn't finished. "Bub," she said—with her thick Albanian accent she called him "Bub"—"get me the food."

"What?" he asked. "What are you going to do with one hundred and twenty-nine airline lunches?"

"They can't use them. We can give them to the poor."

The flight landed and with some reluctance Bob went to the airline officials who were gathered on the tarmac to greet Mother Teresa. They shook hands and he finally asked, "Mother would like to know if she could have the lunches too?" The officials responded, "Of course…anything Mother Teresa wants."

Bob returned to Mother Teresa with the good news. She hardly paused for breath: "Bub, get me the truck."

A few minutes later lanky Bob Macauley was sitting in the passenger seat of a Taca Airlines truck being driven by a nun who was so short that she had to peer between the steering wheel and the dashboard to see. Where were they going? To the poor. She was a terrible driver and he figured it was only by the grace of God that she didn't get in an accident. In half an hour they were in one of Mexico City's desperately poor neighborhoods, handing out airline meals. "Just ask" was the message Bob took from the experience. "It's easy to ask when you're doing it for the poor," Mother Teresa told him. God could give the power to do anything when you were doing it for the people who needed it most.

But it means taking a risk, sticking your neck out and trying something that no one else has tried yet. "No, that's not going to work" or "No, I could never do that" get bumped out of place with a "Yes, and..."

I've mentioned those yellow Post-it notes that I use for scribbling the names of people I've promised to pray for (would that I could remember their names without writing them down but maybe the writing down is part of the prayer process). Did you know they were the project of a 3M inventor who came up with the idea when he was singing in his church choir at North Presbyterian in St. Paul and lost his place in the hymnal for the introit? He had a slip of paper marking the spot but it fell out and fluttered to the floor when he rose to sing. How frustrating. Which page were they on? Which line? Couldn't someone come up with some better way to mark a spot than a loose scrap of paper?

What if that someone were him?

Arthur Fry started by thinking he'd make some sort of self-sticking, removable, hymnal page marker. He had a colleague who'd developed an adhesive that nobody could find any use for because it wouldn't grip permanently. It would hold two pieces of paper together but anybody could easily peel the papers apart. What good was that?

He applied the adhesive to a piece of paper and it stuck in the hymnal all right but it left a residue on the page. (Some of those hymnal pages at North Presbyterian were stuck together for years.) With some experimenting in the lab at 3M Arthur found a way of getting a residue-free glue into the narrow "low tack" range—not too sticky but sticky enough. In due time he had a pad of nice little peel-off bookmarks that he could use in his hymnal.

Then it hit him. Who else would want these things? Had he spent his time developing a failure of a product (at 3M research scientists like Arthur were given the privilege of spending fifteen percent of their time on pet projects)? When he stuck one of them on a report that he had to send to his boss and it came back with an answer scrawled on the same sticky note, it finally occurred to him that this could be more than just a bookmark. You could put the notes on anything—a phone, a refrigerator, a magazine. Stick 'em on and peel 'em off.

It was only when they passed sample pads of the peel-off notes around the office that Arthur had his first indication that he might have a success on his hands. Everybody started coming back for more.

And later, when 3M marketed them to office supply stores, it was only by giving samples for people to use that Post-It notes took off. They were hooked. People didn't know they needed them till they had them in hand. My prayer list sits next to my phone or by my computer or on my desk or gets folded up in my pocket. Until I fill up another Post-it note. Thanks to a choir singer who lost his place in a hymnal—and was convinced there was a better way.

Arthur Fry was lucky to be able to see the success of his creation but that's not always the case. There are times you say "Yes, and…" and then don't know for years—if at all—what God meant when he was moving in your life, when he gave you that nudge and you responded in such good faith. "If they had been thinking of the land they left behind," says the author of the letter of the Hebrews, referring to the faithful of past and present, "they would have had opportunity to return. But as it is, they desire a better country, that is, a heavenly one. Therefore God is not ashamed to be called their God; indeed, he has prepared a city for them" (Hebrews 11:15-16). Hope carries all of us on. It gives us that heavenly city to work for and dream of, that better country. Hope is one of those great gifts we can give each other.

Betty McFarlane remembered the day her mother declared that she was going to be a writer. It was what she felt the Lord was telling her to do. Her great dream. She bought stationery and business cards with her name, address and the words "Writer and Lecturer" confidently printed on them. She cleared a corner in the basement, made a desk by putting a door across two file cabinets and borrowed a typewriter. Most importantly—what Betty couldn't forget—was the box her mother put on the desk. Covered in cream-colored cotton printed with tiny forget-me-nots, it had a pale blue ribbon tied around it and the words "Acceptance Letters."

Betty said, "It must have never occurred to Mama that she might get some rejections."

But before she had the chance to probe too deeply into *Writer's Market* or even finish an article and send it off, her husband left her and Betty's mother was suddenly the sole provider for her children. There was no time for crafting stories for publication. Her writing was limited to the encouraging notes she slipped into lunch boxes and left on dressers for her children.

Betty doesn't remember when her mother put the stationery or the box with its hopeful blue ribbon away. Whenever she'd see her mom sitting down to write, it was more likely a letter to one of her brothers in the service or a card to a friend or a note cheering up a relative. Even after the kids moved out, her mom was busy: caring for her son after a serious car accident, helping her daughter with a baby, taking in Grandpa when he got sick, lending a hand with a neighbor who had no one else to turn to.

After her mother died Betty found the old box with its forget-me-not cover in a cedar chest. To Betty's surprise it was heavy when she lifted it out, the blue ribbon frayed from tying and untying. What would her mom have put inside? Betty opened the box and began to read the "acceptance letters" her mom had saved over the years:

"Thank you, Mom, for your letters," her brother wrote. "I could never have made it through boot camp without them."

"Just a note to tell you how much I appreciated your support…"

"Thank you for writing during those months I was pregnant…"

"Thank you for taking the time to send me the pretty note cards…"

"Your letter came when I was at my lowest point."

"Mama, thank you for your constant support, prayers and love…"

Betty's mother's dream *had* come true in an unexpected way. She had a writing career that was successful beyond her wildest imaginings. The accolades in the box proved it.

I must confess that I have a file in my desk drawer with letters I've collected over the years from friends, strangers, loved ones who have written incredibly kind things I don't want to forget. When I'm feeling rotten or discouraged or wonder if I have done much with my life, I open the file and read. It's like getting a premature eulogy or sitting down at some impossible-to-arrange dinner party with guests from across the years and across the continent, and watching them stand up to say, "Rick, you did all right." I slip the letters back into the file and feel like writing a note myself to someone else, surprising them—I hope—with an unexpected, well-deserved good word.

I remember one Christmas as a kid thumbing through the pile of cards we received, stacks of family photos taken on exotic vacations or pictures of families dressed in red and green and posed in front of a mantel decorated with holly and ivy, everyone smiling and wishing Merry Christmas. But then there'd be a Hallmark card from some person I didn't know, the signature scrawled in a fragile hand with a message saying, "So glad to receive your note. You're so nice to remember me. Merry Christmas to you all!"

"Mom, who's this?" I asked.

"Oh," she said, "she was our house mother in college. I haven't seen her in years but I always send her a card." Or it would be a long-ago babysitter or the woman who retired from the cleaner's or some distant teacher. "I remember visiting her at Christmas once and seeing just a few cards on her bedside table. I thought she should have some more."

The people that need our help are many. Like the young rich man with so many possessions he simply walked away grieving, we can feel so overwhelmed by their needs we want to give up. We do nothing, say nothing. But "Yes, and..." can start with just one small response. A card, a word, a letter, an e-mail, a note, a hospital visit. You'll feel the prompting in your heart and even though you won't know what to say, the words will come. Sometimes just your presence will be enough.

The *Guideposts* story I'm most likely to retell if someone asks me, "What do you do?" or "Where do you work?" and "What kind of stories do you publish?" is one called "Mrs. Lake's Eyes," by an author who asked to remain anonymous. Mrs. Lake was the sixth grade teacher she could never forget, the one who changed her life.

It happened the day of the parent-teacher conferences. Mrs. Lake had set up chairs in the back of the room and as each set of parents came in, she met with them and talked over their child's progress. The girl knew her parents wouldn't show up. They never had. She'd asked them before to come to parent-teacher conferences. She'd brought home notices. Other teachers had made phone calls. Her mother would say, "Yes, we'll try," but didn't come. Some excuse was always made or, worse, nothing was ever said.

How could she explain that to Mrs. Lake? How could she tell this beloved teacher that the reason her parents didn't come to back-to-school night or chaperone field trips or even come by school at the end of the day to pick her up was that they both drank? It was too humiliating. And somehow she feared it was all her fault.

One by one the other students sat with their parents and Mrs. Lake and then returned to their desks. At last it was her turn. With a sinking feeling, she went to face Mrs. Lake. "I'm sorry," she wanted to say, "I told my parents...."

Mrs. Lake took the words out of her mouth. She stood up, folded up the two chairs parents usually sat in, and gestured to the girl to sit in the one chair left. "I know why your parents aren't here," she said. "But I just wanted to tell you all the good things I would have said to them." She went on to give the girl a glowing report.

It was a watershed moment. There would be years before she fully understood and years before she worked it out, but that moment that Mrs. Lake looked her in the eye and said, "I know why your parents aren't here..." was the beginning of healing for her. It was the first time an adult had ever acknowledged that she was not her parents and their problems were not her fault. It was the first glimpse she had of God's love for her. She saw it in Mrs. Lake's eyes.

What would have happened if Mrs. Lake hadn't spoken up? What prompted her to say just the right words? When the story was published, did she see it? (This must be the editor in me talking.) Did she get to find out—as Kevin Felts did—what an influence she'd had? "When you give alms, do not let your left hand know what your right hand is doing, so that your alms may be done in secret; and your Father who sees in secret will reward you," Jesus said (Matthew 6:3-4). When we act nobly it is all the nobler if we don't expect thanks or rewards for it. The same is true for our prayer life; the best part of it is done in secret. As Jesus says a few verses later: "Whenever you pray, go into your room and shut the door and pray to your Father who is in secret; and your Father who sees in secret will reward you" (Matthew 6:6).

Carol Burnett has often told a story about the man who helped her launch her career. She was a stage-struck drama student at UCLA and performed at a party with some friends at a professor's house in San Diego. Afterward a stranger came up to her, introduced himself, asked her what she hoped to do with her life. Go to New York and be an actress, Carol said. He wondered what was stopping her. She had to admit that she had barely enough money to get home, let alone cross the country. She grew up in a family where, at times, her mother, her grandmother and her sister had all been on welfare. The man said he would be happy to lend her the money to go to New York. A thousand dollars.

"Well, in those days I was pretty innocent," Carol admitted, "but not *that* innocent." She politely refused.

The man was insistent, and just to make clear that he meant well, he introduced Carol to his wife and made the offer again. He had only three conditions: If she were successful, that she repay the loan without interest in five years. That she never reveal his identity. And finally, if she accepted his offer, she was to pass the kindness along, to help some other person in similar circumstances when she was able to.

He told her to think it over and call him. He made the same offer to one of her fellow performers.

The next day, afraid she'd dreamed the whole thing, she called the number he had given, said she had decided to accept the conditions. Both her mother and grandmother had discouraged her, told her to have nothing to do with the man. But she was convinced he was sincere and that this was just the push she needed. She was being guided. If she didn't accept the offer and go to New York, she would regret it for the rest of her life.

She and a friend drove down to the man's office in San Diego, waited for half an hour, were ushered in, received their checks, cashed one of them so they would have enough money to pay for gas to get back to Los Angeles (after a banker's phone call to make sure the check wasn't a forgery), then drove home. Carol used a portion of the funds to get two teeth filled and one extracted—she hadn't been able to afford a dentist. Then she headed for New York.

It was a tough slog, hard to get work, hard to get noticed by agents, hard to get experience, but slowly, surely, she made her way. She let her secret benefactor know how she was doing, but heard very little from him. He continued to insist upon his anonymity and showed no desire to share the spotlight or take any credit.

Five years to the day that she had accepted the loan, Carol Burnett paid the man back. She has kept her pledge never to reveal his identity, throughout a career that went from Broadway to TV to films. As for his provision that she pass the kindness along to others—well, that's been her secret.

"Yes, and..." is what we say. God can be as quick to say it back to us: "Yes, and..." The answers become secrets we're meant to treasure, like Carol Burnett's. Or they become secrets we're meant to give away. "I find it just too hard to get silent and sit and pray," said a musician friend recently, someone who gives generously as a teacher and coach and choir director. "But don't you realize," I said impatiently, "you're praying all the time with all those kind deeds you do." "I'm never sure if it's God speaking or not when I think I get his guidance," another friend said, "and I'm tempted not to do anything." "But, but, but," I sputtered, "how can you know until you act on the guidance?" If you make some terrible mistake, God can help, but if you do nothing, he can do nothing.

We can hesitate, we can back up, we can look the other way, we can postpone, we can be locked in prayer paralysis, but why not take a chance and make a leap of faith? "Yes, and..." What a great way to live.

# Epilogue

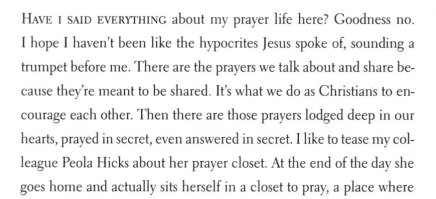

HAVE I SAID EVERYTHING about my prayer life here? Goodness no. I hope I haven't been like the hypocrites Jesus spoke of, sounding a trumpet before me. There are the prayers we talk about and share because they're meant to be shared. It's what we do as Christians to encourage each other. Then there are those prayers lodged deep in our hearts, prayed in secret, even answered in secret. I like to tease my colleague Peola Hicks about her prayer closet. At the end of the day she goes home and actually sits herself in a closet to pray, a place where her daughter and husband won't interrupt her (if they can even find her), a sanctuary of peace and quiet. I tell her she's a closet case.

But Peola has the right idea. I once heard of an alcoholic who would sneak her booze in the closet where she thought no one would notice (she was only fooling herself). When she got sober she went back to that same closet and made it her praying place. And her giving place. It was as though she were rewriting the story of her life, transforming a place of pain through prayer.

Are there really just ten prayers you can't live without? Aren't there more? I believe there are as many prayers as there are people in the world. God has made us all different, each of us unique. The sound I make when I cry out for help is going to be very different from the sound you make. Voices are so unique that on the phone most of us can identify a caller in a word or two, especially when it's someone we love. As a performer on stage I've always been struck by how just a cough or a clearing of the throat from someone I know and love is immediately identifiable. An actor friend said he could tell if his mother was in the audience by the jangle of the charm bracelet she always wore.

Our sounds, our being, our requests, our presence, our needs, our petitions, our exclamations of thanks and praise must be just as identifiable to God and as often anticipated.

Can you live without prayer? You can, but why would you? It's like asking why you would live without love and kindness and hope and faith and good friends and family members who spur you on. Why would you not take advantage of what's freely offered and extravagantly given? Be bold, be playful, be quick, be patient, be thoughtful and then forget all words and thoughts. Just be. Complain all you want about how hard it is but don't say, "I don't know how to pray." Of course you know how. You were made to pray.

# Acknowledgments

NOT LONG AGO, David Morris and I took a long drive to visit John and Elizabeth Sherrill in Massachusetts and we talked a lot about what makes a book work. Would that this were such a book. David, pal, thanks for shepherding this tome through its genesis, creation and any afterlife it has.

My colleagues here at *Guideposts* magazine have to take credit—or blame—for what writer I've become. Edward Grinnan, master editor, has been not only a brilliant teacher over the years but a dear friend. Colleen Hughes reminds me again and again of the tenets of good storytelling. Amy Wong continues to coax me into writing clearly and economically. She also always makes me laugh. I'm especially grateful, Amy, for your eagle eye on this project.

Rebecca Maker offered much help in the generation of this project; Jon Woodhams sent me a crucial help-me-rethink-this-book memo; Marcus Silverman has been an important cheerleader and valued friend. Anne Adriance and Kelly Coyne, thanks for your research and your reminders of the daily place prayer has in people's lives. Kristine Cunningham and Lu Broas, thanks for your marketing genius and getting this book out the door. Anne Simpkinson and Nina Hammerling, you have helped me hone my thoughts again and again as editors of my blog, asking me the crucial question, "What exactly *do* you mean here?" Celeste McCauley, you have often saved me from myself. Mary Lou Carney, you are a great encourager; Nancy Galya, your chocolates and friendship give me fuel.

To our wonderful OurPrayer bunch and Outreach team, you guys really wrote the book on prayer and rewrite it day after day, helping millions. Some of you appear by name here (hi, Peola Hicks; hi, Lemuel Blackett); others of you appear anonymously. Thanks for your good work, Pablo Diaz, Mary Ann Gillespie, Angela Adams, Sandy Wisor, Kelly Mangold, Sabra Ciancanelli, Kathleen Ryan, Donna Marino. I'm with you every Monday morning along with those of us at the table in New York City, particularly our dear Sharon Azar whose experience of prayer is probably more various than anybody's—"with timbrel and dance" as the psalmist says. Rocco Martino, thanks for having confidence in me. May it not be misplaced. My agent, Emma Sweeney, has put my mind at ease too many times. Stacy and Brenda, you saw portions of this in an earlier draft and may you know that your appreciation gave me much courage.

My church, St. Michael's Episcopal, has prayed us through the ups and downs of life for thirty years, God bless you. To the vestry and staff, amen! My men's group buddies Scott, David and Jim, you've been incredible prayer companions over the years. And to the choir, forgive me for all those wrong notes in praise and chant.

My immediate family has endured patiently and heroically their inclusion in my storytelling, particularly my wife, Carol, who politely doesn't challenge my version of things, at least in print. To the boys, Will and Tim, you can do no wrong in my book. To the rest of our large clan, you are constant reiteration of Dad's many blessings.

Rick Thyne and Neil Warren, dear mentors, I hear your voices when I read Paul's passionate words of prayer. Arthur Caliandro, who died just as this book was going to press, Godspeed, you good and faithful servant and prayer friend. Finally, I would like to thank all those people who have told their stories in *Guideposts* and the editors who have made those stories happen. I couldn't improve upon your words.

## Discover More Prayer Resources

To read more from Rick Hamlin, visit his blog guideposts.org/blogs/on-the-journey and on Facebook: Facebook.com/RickHamlinPray.

Visit OurPrayer.org, a community of faith seekers, to submit a prayer request or to sign up for OurPrayer Daily newsletter as well as find free e-books on prayer.

To learn more about other Guideposts publications, including the best-selling devotional *Daily Guideposts*, go to Guideposts.org.

# Questions for Reflection

As you read *10 Prayers You Can't Live Without* by Rick Hamlin, you may find yourself thinking about how you might strengthen your prayers in your walk with God. The following questions can help you put your thinking into action. Consider writing in a journal, or perhaps you'll find these questions helpful for a group discussion about prayer. As you reflect, ask God to help you articulate your answers with clarity and in a way that will bring the greatest impact.

## Chapter One: Pray at Mealtime

1. Was there a special prayer you recited before meals when you were a child? Write down or share a special memory associated with this prayer or with another grace you remember from your youth.

2. What does it mean to bless someone or something? Who has the ability to bless? Why do we refer to the good things in our lives as blessings?

3. How can we use prayer to combat the negative influences in our lives (bad news, critical colleagues, gloomy family members)? Can mealtime graces be about more than food?

4. C. S. Lewis said, "God likes food; he invented hunger." Why do you suppose that is? How are we to honor our God-given need to eat?

## Chapter Two: Prayer as Conversation

1. If you could use only ten words to describe prayer, what would those words be? Has your idea of prayer changed as you matured in your faith?

2. Do you have a special designated place where you pray? Do you think this is important? Why or why not?

3. How do you incorporate prayer into your daily routine? What would you say to those who say they do not have time to pray?

**Chapter Three: Pray for Others**

1. How important do you think it is to pray for other people? Do you believe our prayers have any real impact on their lives?

2. Do you have a prayer list or other aid (such as candles, beads, etc.) that you use to help you remember the ones you want to pray for? When you pray for your loved ones, what do you ask God for? How do you know God is listening to your requests?

3. Have you ever prayed for a stranger? What prompted your action? How did you feel afterward? *we get what we need!*

4. What happens when you don't get what you asked for? What are the benefits of praying for other people?

**Chapter Four: Pray the Lord's Prayer**

1. What is your earliest memory of praying the Lord's Prayer? How often do you pray it? Do you think it is important to pray it every day? Why or why not?

2. Do you think Jesus' disciples were surprised by this simple prayer? How did it differ from the way the Pharisees and other religious leaders of the day offered up their prayers? Can a short prayer be as effective as a long one?

3. Why is this prayer of Jesus spoken in the plural (give *us*, forgive *us*, lead *us*)? Are Christians alone in their efforts to live for God? How

can you be a support to other Christians? How does the Lord's Prayer bind us together?

## Chapter Five: Praying for Forgiveness

1. Write down or share a time when someone hurt your feelings or made you angry. How did you feel? What did you do? What do you think Jesus would have done in that same situation?

2. Why do we find it so hard to forgive each other? How do you feel when you pray, "Forgive us our trespasses as we forgive those who trespass against us"?

3. Can you forgive but not forget? What dangers—spiritual, emotional, physical—are involved with holding on to old hurts?

4. Recall a time when you had to ask someone to forgive you. Is it easier to forgive or to ask for forgiveness?

## Chapter Six: Pray through a Crisis

1. Has there ever been a time in your life when something so terrible happened to you that all you wanted to do was shout "No!"? How do you think God feels when we are too distraught even to pray? How does the Holy Spirit help us in times such as these?

2. How would you explain the nature of God to someone who had had no exposure to religious thought of any kind? Do you believe God gets angry? At what? What is God's most distinguishing, consistent character trait?

3. Why do bad things happen to good people? Is God able to identify with our pain? Why or why not?

4. Is it ever okay to be angry with God? Have you ever been angry with God? Is there a way to constructively use that anger? How do

we resolve feelings of anger or abandonment by God? How can Scripture help us in this?

## Chapter Seven: Sing Your Prayer

1. What role has music played in your faith journey? Write down or share a favorite music-related memory from your past.

2. Look up the words *song* and *sing* in a Bible concordance. Read out loud Scripture related to singing.

3. Do you have a favorite hymn? What about it speaks to your heart and mind? Sing it or read it out loud.

4. Can songs serve as prayers? How? What does it mean to praise God? How do songs help us do this?

## Chapter Eight: A Classic Prayer to Focus Your Thoughts

1. Have you used the "Jesus Prayer" as part of your devotional life? If so, share your experience with it. How could this prayer keep you focused on God throughout the day?

2. Why do you think so many people find this prayer to be powerful and effective? What is the prayer asking? Why is it important to pray this often?

3. Write down or share a time when God asked you to step out of your comfort zone in order to serve God. What gave you the courage to follow through? What feelings surface when you think about surrendering your life completely to God's will?

## Chapter Nine: Pray in Thanksgiving at All Times

1. Gratitude is one of the easiest means of prayer. Why is that? On a scale of one to ten (ten being the highest), how grateful are you on a daily basis? What could you do to improve this score?

2. Have you ever kept a gratitude journal? For the next week, try writing down three things every day for which you're grateful. Then discuss the process with your study group. Was this exercise easy? Difficult? Were you surprised at any of the things you wrote down? Did keeping this journal make you more aware of God's blessings? Is it something you would consider continuing to do?

3. Do you spend more time asking God for things you want or thanking God for things God has given you? How do you think God feels about your answer?

4. The Bible commands us to "give thanks in all circumstances" (1 Thessalonians 5:18). How is this possible? Do you know anyone who continually displays an "attitude of gratitude"?

**Chapter Ten: Pray Yes**

1. When you are faced with a new opportunity or challenge, are you more apt to respond with "yes" or "no"? Why?

2. Write down or share a time when you believe God was using you as an answer to someone's prayer, a time when your "yes" helped build God's kingdom on earth. How do you feel looking back on those events? How has that experience impacted your own spiritual walk?

3. Do you think of prayer as active or passive? Why?

4. Hope is one of the greatest gifts we can give each other. Recall a time when someone helped move you out of despair and hopelessness. What are some practical, specific ways you can help bring hope into your home, your church, your community, your world?

## ABOUT THE AUTHOR

Rick Hamlin is the executive editor of *Guideposts* magazine, where he has worked for more than 25 years. His spiritual memoir, *Finding God on the Train*, was a Book of the Month Club alternate selection and a selection of One Spirit Book Club. He lives with his family in New York City. Visit him at *www.rickhamlin.com*.

Hampton Roads Publishing Company
. . . *for the evolving human spirit*

Hampton Roads Publishing Company
publishes books on a variety of subjects,
including spirituality, health,
and other related topics.

For a copy of our latest trade catalog,
call (978) 465-0504 or visit
our distributor's website at
*www.redwheelweiser.com.*

You can also sign up for our
newsletter and special offers by going to
*www.redwheelweiser.com/newsletter/.*